Private Elisha Stockwell, Jr.
Sees the Civil War

Private
Elisha Stockwell, Jr.
Sees the Civil War

EDITED BY BYRON R. ABERNETHY

NORMAN

UNIVERSITY OF OKLAHOMA PRESS

BY BYRON R. ABERNETHY

Liberty Concepts in Labor Relations
(Washington, 1943)
Private Elisha Stockwell, Jr., Sees the Civil War
(ed.) (Norman, 1958)

Library of Congress Cataloging in Publication Data

Stockwell, Elisha, 1846–1935.
  Private Elisha Stockwell, Jr., sees the Civil War.

  Includes index.
    1. Stockwell, Elisha, 1846–1935. 2. United States—History—Civil War, 1861–1865—Personal narratives. 3. United States. Army. Wisconsin Infantry Regiment, 14th (1862–1865)—Biography. 4. Soldiers—Kansas—Biography. I. Abernethy, Byron R. II. Title.
E601.S87 1985   973.7'81   58–6855

Library of Congress Catalog Card Number: 58–6855

ISBN: 0–8061–1921–7

CONTENTS

ILLUSTRATIONS

INTRODUCTION

Elisha Stockwell, Jr., was born June 28, 1846, at Athol, Massachusetts. When he was three years of age, his parents moved to Beloit, Wisconsin, and a few years later to Alma, Jackson County, Wisconsin. It was here that Elisha, Jr., spent the rest of his childhood and youth until, at the age of fifteen years, he answered President Lincoln's call for volunteers and enlisted in Company I, Fourteenth Wisconsin Volunteer Infantry, February 25, 1862. He was mustered in at Fond du Lac, Wisconsin, left for the front with his company on March 8, 1862, and participated in his first battle, the Battle of Shiloh, April 7, 1862. He received two wounds in this battle, the only injuries which he suffered during the war. He was promoted to corporal March 1, 1865, and was mustered out October 9, 1865, at the end of the war.

While in Wisconsin on furlough, he was married to Miss Katherine Hurley of Milwaukee, Wisconsin, March 14, 1864. After the war they made their home near Alma, Wisconsin, until 1872, when they moved by ox team to Otter Tail County, Minnesota. There they claimed a homestead and built their cabin on the shore of Lake Lizzie, where the town of Dunvilla now stands. After four years, they moved back to Wisconsin in 1876 and made their home on a farm near Black River Falls for the next thirty years.

In 1906, at the age of sixty, Elisha Stockwell sold his farm in Wisconsin, and with his family again pioneered a new area just being settled in western North Dakota. Here Mr. and Mrs. Stockwell spent the rest of their lives, at Beach, North Dakota. Here also a marriage which had lasted nearly sixty-three years was broken by the death of Mrs. Stockwell in 1927. Elisha Stockwell died December 29, 1935, at the age of eighty-nine years and six months, almost seventy-four years after he had enlisted with Company I. He was the last survivor of Company I, and the next to the last survivor of his regiment, only R. A. Spieck of his regiment still living at that time.

Following the death of Mrs. Stockwell in 1927, Mr. Stockwell was persuaded to attempt to tell the story of his Civil War experiences for his family. Thus, at the age of eighty-one, he began writing his Civil War memoirs. They were written entirely from memory, sixty-three years after many of the events had taken place. As he said, he had no way to verify dates and remembered only what impressed him most. Moreover, most of the work was done at a time when cataracts had robbed him of his sight, and, being unable to see the lines on his paper, he used a piece of wood, the width of the space between two lines, to write against, turning it over after each line, to guide his writing.

The memoirs in his longhand were not readily available to more than a few persons. Even within his own family, only a few ever saw them, and fewer still ever tried to read them. They were kept by one of his daughters, Mrs. M. F. Smith, who in 1951 gave them to me to be typed and put in easily accessible form for all the members of the family. As is the case with most good intentions, my plan to start the work on these memoirs promptly was delayed by the press of other, and what seemed more urgent, matters, until an illness which freed me from daily responsibilities of a job during the greater part of two years afforded the opportunity of putting the memoirs in readable shape.

The memoirs, as Elisha Stockwell completed them, had no chapters, very few paragraph breaks, and little punctuation; but in spite of these conditions and the handicap under which he wrote, the manuscript was surprisingly readable. While I have given his work its present mechanical structure, it is hardly accurate to call what I did an editing of his manuscript. The work remains the work of Elisha Stockwell throughout. The words and sentence construction, with very few changes, are his. My part has been limited to breaking the material into chapters and paragraphs and adding punctuation, with an occasional grammatical correction, such as making subject and verb agree in number. The modifications which I have made in his manuscript have been only those which seemed necessary to facilitate the reading of the story. Throughout, my aim has been to leave this the narrative of Elisha Stockwell, just as he told it. The style remains his, not mine.

The footnotes are all mine. Elisha Stockwell had none in his manuscript. When I was pursuing my original intention of preparing it for private publication for members of the Stockwell family, I inserted the notes to clarify the text and to provide the reader with additional information which might be helpful and interesting.

This has been a pleasant task, and often, as I worked at it, I wished that it were possible to sit with Mr. Stockwell again and persuade him to enlarge on his personal reactions to the political issues of that day, which he assiduously avoided throughout the manuscript, as well as to prompt him to recount the many additional incidents which he used to relate, but which he neglected to record.

It has been particularly fascinating to read the accounts written by Grant, Sherman, and others, of the same battles he describes. Elisha Stockwell's stories of the battles, sieges of forts, and campaigns acquire enhanced charm as the view of a lone private in the midst of the same scenes and events described elsewhere by military commanders and historians. The reader will find a comparison on his own part rewarding indeed. Compare, for example, Stockwell's account of the death of General McPherson near Atlanta (in Chapter IV) with General Sherman's description of the same event in his *Personal Memoirs*. Edgar Houghton's "History of Company I" in the *Wisconsin Magazine of History* (September, 1927) also makes interesting reading in comparison with Stockwell's memoirs.

Here is a private's-eye-view of great historical events as they took place, and of history as it was made by the little men, who after all are the real makers of history. Here one sees a teen-age boy experiencing war at Shiloh; wandering around the battlefields before Atlanta amid a shower of cannon balls; becoming impatient with his treatment under Sherman, and simply decamping to rejoin his own regiment in Tennessee. Here one sees what it was that impressed a common soldier during that most tragic experience of the American people, the American Civil War.

BYRON R. ABERNETHY

Lubbock, Texas

Private Elisha Stockwell, Jr.
Sees the Civil War

CHAPTER I

A BOY OF FIFTEEN YEARS GOES TO WAR

In the summer of 1861 I was fifteen years old, could rake and bind and keep up with the men. (They cut the grain with cradles then.) I got fifty cents a day and a man one dollar, but my father collected my wages as he was a very poor man.

In September I was helping a neighbor stack grain and we heard there was going to be a war meeting at our little log school house.[1] I went to the meeting, and when they called for volunteers, Harrison Maxon, Edgar Houghton, and myself put our names down. There were nineteen that afterwards enlisted from the town of Alma, Jackson County, Wisconsin, in the same company, but they are all dead but us three.[2] Harrison

[1] At Alma, Wisconsin. Lincoln had been inaugurated as president of the United States on March 4, 1861. The Confederate States had been organized, a provisional constitution adopted, Jefferson Davis selected as provisional president, and secession declared in February preceding Lincoln's inauguration. Fort Sumter had been attacked on April 12, Lincoln had called for 75,000 volunteers on April 15, and by May of that year war had become a reality.

[2] This was written in 1927. In September, 1927, *The Wisconsin Magazine of History* (Vol. XI, No. 1) published a "History of Company I," by Edgar P. Houghton, which was evidently written between 1905 and 1909, as Mr. Houghton said he was writing forty-four years after the time of which he wrote—1861 to 1865. In his "History of Company I," Edgar Houghton tells several incidents

Maxon lives at Humbird, Wisconsin, and E. P. Houghton at Puyallup, Washington. Edgar was one year and five months older than I was and Maxon some six years older than I was.

My father was there and objected to my going, so they scratched my name out, which humiliated me somewhat. My sister gave me a severe calling down the first time I saw her for exposing my ignorance before the public, and called me a little snotty boy, which raised my anger. I told her, "Never mind, I'll go and show you that I am not the little boy you think I am."

---

also related in these memoirs. In his article he singles out Elisha Stockwell, J. W. Ferguson, and George P. King for special treatment as the three youngest soldiers in the company, devoting a paragraph to each.

Of Elisha Stockwell, he said (pp. 47–48): "Stockwell wrote his name on the list at a war meeting in the log schoolhouse at Alma in September, '61, but his father would not consent to his enlisting at that time and the company went to Fond du Lac without him. But he did not give up: the following February he drove his father's ox team into Black River Falls with a load of charcoal and left the team on the street, walked to Sparta, took the train from there to Fond du Lac, and joined the company just before we left the state. He was wounded twice at the battle of Shiloh, first slightly in the shoulder with musket-ball, and later he was hit on the arm with canister shot. Although it did not break the skin his arm became so badly swollen that he could not use it and upon complaining to the lieutenant that he could not load his gun, he was ordered to go to the rear. After the battle he said he was disappointed because so many of the rebels got away, as he had supposed that when the battle opened they kept on firing until all on one side or the other were killed."

This article also contains a roster of the members of Company I, which provides some military records of persons referred to in these memoirs. Subsequent notes identifying individuals are taken from this roster. These and other references to this work are hereinafter cited merely as "Houghton."

Then she began to coax me, and my mother began too. I was always easily coaxed, so I promised not to go if Father would let me go to school that winter. Father wasn't present at that time and never broached the subject to me at any time, but he took a contract to burn charcoal fifteen miles from home to pay for a new wagon. (The blacksmiths used charcoal in those days.) He said if I would help him get the pit up I could then go to school.

We had an ox team that I could drive as well as a man. In February, 1862, I was up home after supplies, as we camped at the coal pit. I heard Daniel Houghton (who was Edgar's father and in the same company and was in camp at Fond du Lac, Wisconsin) was home on furlough. I went and saw him and told him I wanted to go back with him. He asked if my father had consented to my going, and said he could come and take me out if I went without his consent. But I told him I was bound to go, and if he wouldn't help me, I would go alone and have to foot it, as I couldn't get money to pay my fare on the railroad. He said if I was bound to go, he would see me through, and would be at the hotel at Black River Falls Sunday noon. I hauled the coal to Black River Falls, and my brother-in-law worked in the shop where I delivered it.

I told my father I heard there was going to be a Dutch dance Sunday night and I wanted to go and see it, as I had never seen one. He said he hadn't any money, but that I might go. So he helped me load a load of coal.

5

I unloaded it at the blacksmith shop, drove up to my brother-in-law's, tied the oxen to the fence, and went in and saw my sister a few minutes. I told her I had to go down town. She said, "Hurry back, for dinner will soon be ready." But I didn't get back for two years.

I saw Mr. Houghton, and told him I would walk on slow until he overtook me. So I didn't get any dinner that day. We had to walk to Sparta to get to the railroad, some twenty-five miles. But we stopped at Pine Hill, some twelve miles, and got our supper, and the landlord said he had to go to Sparta the next day, but would hitch up and take us that night as we had to be there early the next morning to catch the train.

We got to camp the next day, and Edgar was glad to see me as we were great chums and had been together a good deal the last six years. (Will say here he writes to me one month and I to him the next month.) Mr. Houghton told the captain the circumstances, and the captain got me in by my lying a little, as I told the recruiting officer I didn't know just how old I was but thought I was eighteen. He didn't measure my height, but called me five feet, five inches high. I wasn't that tall two years later when I re-enlisted, but they let it go, so the records show that as my height.

I enlisted the twenty-fifth of February, 1862, and got my uniform. One of the company was known as Curly. He was a big husky man and quite handy with his fists. He said he had to try all recruits to see if they could fight, and proceeded to cuff me around until I got quite enough of that play. I told him I didn't enlist to fight that way, but if he would get his gun and go outside of the camp, we would stand thirty or forty rods apart, and I thought I could convince him that I could shoot as well as he could. He turned it off as a joke and said he guessed I would pass. I never liked him after that, but he never bothered me again.

We were quartered in Sibley tents, which were large round tents that were pegged to the ground and ran up to a peak some ten or twelve feet high, held up by a center pole in the middle, set on a tripod about four feet high with three legs that could be spread out or closed up to take the sag out when dry or loosen it when wet. The tent was made of heavy ducking, had an opening at the top about two feet across and was round, and had an opening in one side for a door that closed with a flap and strings to tie it. It had a small sheet-iron stove to warm it while we were at Fond du Lac, but the stoves were left there. On cold nights we took turns keeping fire in them. There were fourteen to sixteen men in a tent. We had straw to lay on while at Fond du Lac, and were quite comfortable, but the ground was our bed after that.

One of the objections my mother had to my going was that I was a sleepyhead. When I was tired or had been broken of my rest the night before, and I got to sleep, they couldn't wake me up until I had my sleep out. It troubled me very badly, but Ed and Hat, as I called them, knew of my failing. We had to answer at nine o'clock roll call in the evening. The penalty for failure to answer was extra duty. The first morning I told them I would be for extra duty as I didn't answer roll call last night, but they said I did answer roll call. They said that Ed called, "Come, Lish, to roll call," and I took my place in the ranks and answered when my name was called, and answered a good many times in my sleep. But the boys found out how to awaken me by touching me lightly and speaking just above a whisper and I would be wide awake; but I came near getting in trouble several times during my service.

There were nearly all big men in my company, and one said it was a disgrace to take such little boys as Jim Ferguson and me in the company. But the first hard march we were on I saw him played out and laying beside the road, and when we went into camp that night there were four privates to stack arms and Jim and I were two of them. Jimmie was a month older than I was. The big man was reduced to a skeleton with chronic diarrhea and got discharged before his first year's service was out.[3]

Several enlisted about the time I did. We were called the awkward squad and drilled by ourselves in the facings and manual of arms. One, Ned Bowen, came in after I did. He was a little stub of an Irishman, and the poorest material for a soldier that I ever saw. He

[3] Ferguson also enlisted at the age of fifteen. Edgar Houghton says of him (p. 47), "Ferguson went out with the company and came back with it, missing very few turns of duty in four years' service, as his health and grit were both good."

had never had a gun in his hands, and couldn't even learn to keep step or the manual of arms. All he was good for was to build breastworks and amuse the rest of the boys. Will speak of him later if I ever finish this.

We left for the front the eighth of March,[4] by rail to Chicago. We marched from one depot to the other in Chicago, and the mud and slush was shoe deep in the streets. It seemed to me that we marched over the biggest part of the city. We had a fine band of fife and drums and were a big regiment of big men, mostly from the logging camps, and rafts of men from northern Wisconsin. Will say here that was the first band of fife and drum I ever heard, and I thought it the finest music. I still like to hear it.

We boarded the cars for Alton, Illinois, and there took a steamboat to St. Louis, Missouri. When we came to where the Missouri River empties into the Mississippi, we could see the different-colored water a mile ahead, as the Missouri is very muddy. It was a long way before the waters mixed, so it looked like two rivers running side by side.

We didn't know where we were going, as a soldier isn't supposed to know any more than a mule, but has to obey orders. But we landed at St. Louis and went on shore, and marched up through the city with fixed bayonets, colors flying and band playing. As our regiment was nearly all big men and nearly 1,000 strong I thought it a grand sight, but the people on the streets

[4] 1862.

9

didn't stop to look at us. I supposed they were mostly Rebels and didn't care to see us or show their fear.

We marched out to Benton Barracks and pitched our tents inside a big enclosure with a high, tight board fence. It was very muddy and rained a good deal while we were there. We drew our mule teams and wagons there, six mules to a wagon. I understood they were three years old and had never had a hand laid on them. They were mostly bay or brown, but one team of six mules was pure white, well matched, and were with us to the end of the war. They were left at Madison and were used as ambulance teams the last I knew of them. They were a nice team.

I thought I was so far from home that Father couldn't come after me so I wrote to Mother, and I wrote to her regularly when I could while in the service.[5] I also got my picture taken and sent to my Grandfather Stockwell, who lived in Massachusetts. This was the first picture I had ever had taken. It was a tintype, and I have it now.

We drilled some while here, but I was in the awkward squad yet and don't remember of being on company drill until after the Battle of Shiloh.

About the twenty-eighth of March we boarded a steamboat and started down the river for Dixie Land.[6] The first stop was at Cairo, Illinois. We got our first

[5] See Appendix for some of the letters he wrote home while in the service.
[6] Edgar Houghton (p. 27) said they left on March 23 and arrived at Savannah, Tennessee, on March 28.

hardtack on the steamboat from Alton to St. Louis. It was piled on a table on the lower deck with the strongest cheese I ever ate. Everyone helped himself to what he liked best. I liked the hardtack and never got tired of it. Also on this trip we got bacon, or "sow bosom," as the boys called it. We drank river water to wash it down.

From Cairo we went up the Ohio, thence up the Tennessee to Savannah, Tennessee, where we landed and went into camp at the edge of town.[7] We got a call for picket duty, and were told anyone could volunteer if he wanted to. I with others volunteered, and Sergeant Mike Higgins[8] went with us. He had been in the regular army five years and knew the drill from A to Z. He was a model soldier and a good instructor. He was very emphatic in giving instructions and I never forgot what he told me.

He posted me and Nels Osgood[9] at the forks of the road, Nels to watch the left hand road and I the right hand. We were to lay down flat on our stomachs and keep close watch, as they expected an attack at any time.

He told us what to do if the grand rounds came, or anyone else. We were not to know anyone until they gave the countersign, which was never spoken above a whisper, and were never to let anyone put their hands

[7] Grant was maintaining his headquarters at Savannah at this time.

[8] Michael Higgins, Black River Falls, Jackson County, enlisted November 15, 1861. Houghton, p. 40.

[9] Nelson Osgood, Neillsville, Clark County, enlisted November 17, 1861; died August 27, 1863, Natchez, Mississippi, disease. Houghton, p. 41.

on our guns while on guard duty at any time. The grand rounds might come at any time, and might not come at all. They were to see that the guards were efficient and safe, as the whole army depended on the picket to give the alarm in case of attack by the enemy. He didn't tell us that the grand rounds might come from any direction.

It was a nice moonlight night and very still. The road was dry and dusty. The reserve was some forty rods back. There was thick timber all around us. This was the first guard duty I had ever done. We had lain there an hour or so when we heard a saber tinkle against a spur. We both sprang to our feet and yelled, "Halt," as there were about ten mounted men close to us in our rear. They halted.

I waited for Nels to challenge them, but as he didn't, I called, "Who goes there?"

They answered, "Grand rounds with the countersign."

I said, "Halt grand rounds, dismount one and advance with the countersign."

It was a brigadier general that came. I halted him when he got within six feet. He stood there without giving the countersign, so I told him to give me the countersign. He put his hand out to push my gun aside as I had it at a charge bayonet, but I slapped his arm with the bayonet, and told him to keep his hands off my gun. He said he had to get up so as to whisper it in my ear.

I said, "You lean over the point of that bayonet and whisper it." So he leaned quite heavily against the bayonet, and gave a false countersign.

I stepped back a little and told him, "Rightabout—face! Mark time, double quick, march!"

He obeyed, but wanted to know what was wrong, and tried to bluff me, said I could see he was a Union officer. But I told him to do just as I told him and he was all right, but if he made a false move, I would stick the bayonet through him. I told Nels to call the sergeant. It seemed to me the sergeant wasn't in a hurry to get there, and that fellow was puffing like a steam engine. The sergeant took them back to the reserve where there was a fire. The sergeant praised me for doing as I did, said if I hadn't done as I did, they would have put me in the guardhouse, which I was mortally afraid of. I was well pleased with myself, and I suspected afterwards that the sergeant had directed him to me as I was a greenhorn, and they must have come by the reserve. I didn't have to drill with the awkward squad after that.

On Sunday morning, April 6, 1862, I was on camp guard, and a little after sunrise, heard musket firing up the river toward Pittsburg Landing, just a shot now and then. I could just hear it faintly as it was some twelve miles off, but soon it was thicker, at times almost a roar. Soon a lot of men came out to the guard line to listen, as they could hear it plainer out of the confusion of the camp.[10]

[10] While Stockwell does not himself identify it as such, it is clear

It must have been an hour before we heard a cannon shot, but we knew a fight was on before that, as General Nelson's division of General Buell's army had camped a little below us the night before, and were soon marching by us nearly on the double quick.

About ten o'clock our colonel called, "Attention men!" and said he had permission to go up, and asked if we wanted to go. It seemed to me as if everyone shouted yes. I kept my mouth shut tight, but I knew I would have to go with the crowd. I felt I would just as soon stay where we were.

We were soon ready to go. We rolled our blankets up (each had a wool and oilcloth blanket), with the oilcloth on the outside, tied the two ends together, and put the roll over our heads and across the left shoulder, took our canteens and haversack, and left the camp in charge of the men that were on the sick list and excused from duty.

It was getting dark before the boat came down the river with a lot of soldiers on it from different regiments. It was said they had compelled the captain of the boat to run down with them. Anyway they were thoroughly whipped—said they were all that was left

---

that this was the beginning of the Battle of Shiloh. The deployment of Nelson's division of Buell's army, the dates involved, the location, the reference to the gunboats *Lexington* and *Tyler*, the spending of the night in the woods in the rain, and the official casualty list for the Battle of Shiloh, including the official record of Stockwell's being wounded, all make clear that it is the Battle of Shiloh with which his narrative deals during the rest of this chapter.

of their regiments. They had to take a lot of abuse from our boys, and had to go back with us. It was thought the captain of that boat was as anxious to go down the river as the soldiers he had with him, as there were two gunboats just above the Landing, the *Lexington* and *Tyler*, which he could have signaled to for aid.

We got up to the Landing about eleven o'clock at night. All was quiet except that those gunboats threw a shell over into the woods at regular intervals of about fifteen minutes. We got off the steamboat and marched to the top of the hill, filed off the road in among some mule barns and wagons, and there we stood in a cold, drizzly rain until daylight.[11] I put my blanket over my shoulders, stuck my bayonet in the ground, leaned my chin on the butt of my gun, and slept standing up, the same as the mules did around me.

As soon as it began to get light, the mules sounded the reveille and woke me up. The rain had passed, and it was clear and bright. We marched out from the teams and rolled up our blankets. Each company piled its blankets and haversacks in piles and left a man to guard them. Ned Bowen was left to guard my company's pile, and we started for the front.

The first dead man we saw was a short distance from

[11] General Grant comments on this rain as follows: "During the night rain fell in torrents and our troops were exposed to the storm without shelter." Grant made his headquarters that same night "under a tree a few hundred yards back from the river bank." U. S. Grant, *Personal Memoirs* (New York, Vol. I, 1885; Vol. II, 1886), I, 349.

the clearing. He was leaning back against a big tree as if asleep, but his intestines were all over his legs and several times their natural size. I didn't look at him the second time as it made me deathly sick. A little farther on we saw lots of dead men scattered through the woods where they had fallen the day before. These were all dressed in blue, but a little farther were some with butternut uniforms mixed among the blue and a little farther nearly all had the butternut uniforms.

I was busy with my thoughts and feelings when Sergeant Johnnie Rockwood[12] said, "Boys, what makes you so quiet?" No one answered, and I began to look at the others. All in sight were pale as ghosts, but Rockwood had considerable color in his face. I know my face was as white as anyone's. But John Rockwood had been in the three months' service and had been under fire. If he had known what was in store for him that day, I don't think he would have laughed at the rest of us. He was shot through the wrist, and the lieutenant asked him if he wanted help to get back to the ambulance. He said no he could get back alone, but didn't go but a short distance when another ball killed him.

Just as Rockwood was laughing at us, Ned Bowen, who had been left to guard the company blankets, overtook us. The lieutenant asked him why he didn't stay and guard the blankets. He said he wasn't going to stay there to be taken prisoner, so they let him go with us.

[12] John G. Rockwood, Black River Falls, Jackson County, enlisted November 18, 1861; killed in action April 7, 1862, Shiloh, Tennessee. Houghton, p. 41.

We were formed in a line of battle to the left of a battery of light artillery, and were ordered to lie down. Lieutenant John Kittinger[13] was in command of the company that day. He was an elderly man, but brave and kind to his men, and a good commander. He said after the battle he counted us as we lay there. There were fifty some odd, have forgotten the exact number,[14] but he said we lost 40 per cent killed and wounded that day.

Ned Bowen was at my left and Curly, who boxed my ears at Fond du Lac, was my right hand man. When the Rebel shells began to fly over our heads, I noticed he stuck his nose into the mud the same as the rest of us, until Rockwood laughed again and said, "Those are going over the tree tops; if they weren't they would hit some of them." The most of us then sat up and quit dodging, but Ned was saying his prayers and trembled like a leaf, and an elderly German, John Schnider,[15] was just as badly scared as Ned.

[13] John Kittinger, Alma, Jackson County, enlisted October 19, 1861, and elected first lieutenant, commissioned November 10, 1861; resigned May 5, 1862. Houghton, p. 38.

[14] Edgar Houghton reports that Lieutenant Kittinger said there were just fifty. He also records eight of the company killed and eleven, including Elisha Stockwell, wounded. He reports that of the eleven wounded only four ever returned to duty with the company. The four who returned to duty apparently were Elisha Stockwell, George Reeder, Nathan Clapp, and either Stanley Parker or Frederick Yonkey. It appears that of the latter two it was more likely Stanley Parker who returned. He died of disease at Hamburg, Tennessee, August 3, 1862. Yonkey died of disease at Keokuk, Iowa, August 14, 1862. The other three went through the remainder of the war. Houghton, p. 30.

[15] From Neillsville, Clark County; deserted February 25, 1864. Houghton, p. 39.

We were not to shoot until ordered to, as Company A was out in front as skirmishers. When they came back they were on the jump, and the bullets began to zip around us. Ned and Schnider thought they were Rebs, and I held Ned's gun up and Curly did Schnider's, as it was no use to talk to them.

It was open timber where we lay, but a little way in front the underbrush was quite thick, so we couldn't see but a short distance. We were ordered to fire, and as soon as I let go of Ned's gun, he stuck it up in the air, shut both eyes, and fired at the tree tops, and Schnider did the same. But Schnider was in rear rank behind Curly and he cut a lock of Curly's hair off just above his ear, and burned his neck. I thought Curly was going to strike him with his gun. He told him, "You might have killed me." And Schnider said, "Makes me not much difference, I not like you very well anyhow." So Curly made him go ahead of him, and none of us saw Ned or Schnider again that day.

I want to say, as we lay there and the shells were flying over us, my thoughts went back to my home, and I thought what a foolish boy I was to run away to get into such a mess as I was in. I would have been glad to have seen my father coming after me.

It is very trying to one's nerves to lay under fire and not be able to do anything in return. But as soon as we were ordered forward, the fear left me, and I went forward with a will, certain we would do them up in a hurry and have this over with.

The Battle of Shiloh

Charge and taking of a New Orleans battery by the Four-teenth Regiment, Wisconsin Volunteers, Monday, April 7, 1862. From a lithograph of a sketch by A. E. Mathews.

The Gunboats *Tyler* and *Lexington*

That supported the Union effort at Shiloh by firing up a ravine back of Pittsburg landing. From a lithograph of a sketch by A. E. Mathews.

We were going down hill when someone hit me in the back with his bayonet quite severely. As I supposed it was carelessness, I turned around to give him a piece of my mind, but there lay the poor fellow shot in the forehead. He was drawing his knees up toward his head, also his hands toward his breast, and the blood spurting from the hole in his forehead. I turned and went on.

We had lost all formation, and were rushing down the road like a mob. When we got to the foot of the hill, there was a small stream of water from the rain of the night before. We stopped there and I got behind a small tree. I could see the little puffs of smoke at the top of the hill on the other side some forty rods from us, and I shot at those puffs. The brush was so thick I couldn't see the Rebs, but loaded and fired at the smoke until a grape shot came through the tree and knocked me flat as I was putting the cap on my gun. I thought my arm was gone, but I rolled on my right side and looked at my arm and couldn't see anything wrong with it, so got to my feet with gun in my hands and saw the Rebs coming down hill just like we had

The road was full for several rods, and I shot for the middle of the crowd and began loading. But as they were getting so close, I looked behind me to see what the rest were doing. I saw the colors going out of sight over the hill, and only two of our men in sight. As I started to run, I heard several shout, "Halt!" But I knew it was the Rebs, and I hadn't any thought of obeying them. I don't think they were over six rods from me.

I didn't think they might kill me, but dreaded to be taken prisoner.

The ground looked queer, as though it was boiling, but I didn't think what the cause was until afterwards. I saw a line of men to my left going the same way I was, and some ahead of me. At that instant the bullet cut across my right shoulder, and it burned like a red hot iron. My first thought was my clothes were afire, and I grabbed it with my left hand, and turned my face to the right. I saw John Rhodus[16] behind a big tree and laughing as though he saw something funny, which riled my temper, but I didn't have time to argue with him.

I was going all this time, and I began to realize that the Rebs were shooting at me. I didn't see anything more until I got to the top of the hill. (It couldn't be called a hill, but was quite an up grade.) There I saw the regiment forming in line, the officers hollering, "Fall in! Fall in!" I took my place in the front rank, and my left arm began to come to its feeling. It hurt me quite bad and I was trying to raise it up, but couldn't raise it to my head. I thought, "What will I do if we get to fighting with the bayonet," as I supposed we were about to do.

At that moment the lieutenant touched me on the shoulder and asked what was the matter. I showed him where the canister shot had hit my arm. It was half-

16 John W. Rhodus, Neillsville, Clark County, enlisted November 7, 1861. Houghton, p. 41.

way between the elbow and shoulder, had burned the wool on my blouse down to the threads and showed plain as long as I had it, which was several months. The boys said I ought to send it home, but someone took it out of my tent, and I never saw it again.

The lieutenant told me to get behind a tree or stump until they made that charge, and then go to the Landing. I was as tickled as a boy let out of school. I got behind a stump, but hadn't been there but a moment when a man from another company came along and asked me if I could help him back. He was wounded in the foot—looked like it was quite bad. So I helped him back to the ambulance, and I went on to the Landing alone.

I left my gun and belts with my blankets and haversack, took my canteen, and started toward the river to get some water. I hadn't gone far when I heard someone call my name. I turned back and there lay four of my company. One was hit in the groin and in awful pain. They asked me if I could get them water. I took their canteens and filled them at a nice spring about halfway down the hill, and got my blankets, spread them on the ground, and helped them onto them. They were put on a steamboat that night and I never saw my blankets again. The boy that was wounded in the groin died, but the others recovered.

We saw on our way out to the front some of the effects of the shells from the gunboats. The Rebs had taken possession of a camp that belonged to our troops.

They were Sibley tents which I have described. They had spread an oilcloth on the ground, and had a candle with a bayonet for a candlestick which was stuck in the ground. There were four of them playing cards, and all of them were dead. Each had three cards in his left hand and the four cards lay in the middle of the blanket. The tent was blown to atoms.

That night I got into a Sibley tent that was full of wounded, but with room next the door where I lay with my clothes on. I slept very sound the fore part of the night, but there was a big German the other side of the door, who made a big noise. He was wounded in the leg, a flesh wound. The doctor dressed his wound the first one, and went on around the tent.

We lay with our feet toward the center of the tent, and across, opposite me, was a slim boy of about my age. He was sitting up with his face down as if looking at the ground. When the doctor came to him and asked him where he was wounded, he looked up but didn't say anything. He was shot just below the left eye and close to the nose. He bent his head over, and put his finger on the back of his neck. The doctor took his knife and cut the ball out and never a whimper out of that boy. When he came to me, I showed him my arm. He wanted to know what position I was in, and said my body saved my arm as it would have broken it if it had been out from my body.

I found my company near by, and John Rhodus told me the Rebs can never catch you. He said I ran over two dead men and a dead horse. He said he couldn't have helped laughing if he had known I would be killed, and he thought I surely would be. So I went out and there was a dead horse, but the men had been removed. I went and saw the tree that had saved my life, and the battery that our regiment had taken, sitting where the Rebs were driven away from it, as their horses were nearly all killed. It was said to be a New Orleans battery and there was a good many dead Rebs on both sides of it.

Ned Bowen and Schnider came to the regiment the next day after the battle. Ned had lost his ramrod and had his gun half-full of cartridges. One of the boys took out the loads and found he had put the ball down first.

CHAPTER II

PICKET DUTY
AT PITTSBURG LANDING AND CORINTH

We were provost guards at the Landing for several months after the Battle of Shiloh.[1] The supplies for the army that advanced on Corinth about twenty-five miles distant were landed here from the steamboats and were hauled out by mule teams. It was a very busy place. The teams went down the hill on one road and up the hill by another at the lower end of the landing. To keep the soldiers from getting in the way, they put a line of guards at the top of the hill. I came on the road going down, with orders not to let anyone go down without a pass. Soon a general and escort came and I saluted. He answered, and I said, "Halt!" but he didn't stop. So I stepped into the road, fetched my gun to charge bayonet, and said, "Halt" in a louder tone.

He stopped very suddenly, grabbed for the holster with his right hand as though to draw his revolver, and

[1] The company was on provost duty at Pittsburg Landing until July 23, 1862; then on similar duty at Hamburg, Tennessee, until August 23, 1862, when the regiment was sent to Corinth, Mississippi, "assigned to the second brigade of McArthur's division, and took part in the battles of Iuka and Corinth." Houghton, p. 31.

24

turned very white in the face. Then he asked me, "What are your orders?"

"My orders are not to let anyone pass without a pass signed by General Halleck, General Grant, or the Provost Marshal."

He says, "I am General Halleck."

I replied, "I don't know you, but you can't pass without a pass."

He said, "Call the corporal."

"I don't need him," I said.

Then he says, "Where is he?"

"I don't know."

Then he rode to the next guard and asked him, "Where is the corporal?" He pointed off a few rods away. As he rode off he said, "I'll have that man in the guardhouse."

He rode to the corporal, and from there to the colonel's tent. He stood there some time but finally rode off, and I never saw him again. Sergeant Higgins had a big laugh when he heard of it, but told me I did just right.

One day George Reeder asked me if I had been across the river. I said no. He had a skiff, and we went over. We made the boat fast and went up the bank. There was a fringe of trees, then an open space. Some eight or ten rods from us was a young man with a U. S. Springfield gun at his shoulder, and some twenty feet beyond was a big Negro who saw us coming and stood his ground. Reeder took the gun and asked where he

got it. He said he picked it up on the battlefield, and
that the Negro belonged to his neighbor and had run
away. We told the Negro we couldn't protect him,
that his master could come and take him out of camp.
But we ought to have taken that fellow and told the
officers how we had found him, as I believe he was a spy.
We let him go, but he tied the Negro's hands behind
his back as we took the gun to camp with us.

Soon after the battle, Governor Harvey of Wisconsin came down to look after the welfare of Wisconsin
soldiers. I didn't see him as I was on guard duty, but
he gave the boys quite a speech, and took one of the
cannon our regiment had captured—the one Lieutenant
Staley spiked[2]—and started back to Wisconsin with it.
The boat stopped at Savannah twelve miles below, and
he went to step on another steamer that lay alongside,
missed his footing, fell in the river, and was drowned.
A detail from our regiment went down and found his
body several miles below Savannah among some drift-
wood.[3] His body with the cannon was taken to Wisconsin. The last time I was in Madison, about twenty-

[2] Lieutenant Staley was with Company D, the La Crosse Company. Company D and Company I were both companies of the same
regiment, the Fourteenth Wisconsin Volunteers, and together
charged the New Orleans battery from which this gun was seized.
This battery was taken after Stockwell was wounded and sent to
the rear, however. Therefore, Stockwell did not personally partici-
pate in his company's seizing of the battery.

[3] E. B. Quiner gives a somewhat different version of the finding
of Governor Harvey's body, but does tell of "a guard of honor con-
sisting of twenty soldiers of the Fourteenth Regiment" accompany-

five years ago, I saw the gun on the capitol grounds, the spike still in it.

I, with others, took a batch of prisoners back to St. Louis. One of them jumped into the river one dark night. They got out a boat and torch light but didn't find him. Some of the other prisoners said he had told them we wouldn't get him to a Northern prison.

At St. Louis, Ed and I walked up town a way and a good many wanted to know if that was a bullet hole in my coat. I let them see it, and I attracted more attention than the whole regiment had a month before.

We went back to the steamboat that took us back to Pittsburg Landing. I went back of the boilers, gaping around like the country Jake I was. I heard someone say, "You are Add Stockwell's brother." I looked behind me, but saw no one, so started on, when the same voice repeated, "You are Add Stockwell's brother." I went back in the direction the voice came from, and a fellow backed out of the big piston box that he was cleaning, and laughed at me.

ing the body to Cairo on the steamer *La Crosse*. According to Quiner, the body was discovered by some children about sixty miles below Savannah and was pulled out of the river by a Negro man who joined the children in robbing the body and returning it to the river. A white man, hearing of the incident, had the body again removed from the river and buried. Then, when it was determined from papers found on the body that the dead man was Governor Harvey, the valuables taken were recovered, the captain of a passing steamer was informed, and the body was disinterred and returned to Wisconsin. Edwin Bentlee Quiner, *Military History of Wisconsin: A Record of the Civil and Military Patriotism in the War for the Union* (Chicago, 1866), 120–21.

I said, "Who are you? I don't remember that I ever saw you."

He said, "No, you never did, and I never saw you before, but I saw your sister when on vacation, at a dance. My name is Will Hamilton." His father's farm joined my father's. He was assistant engineer, and he took me to the cook, and told him to give me my meals while I was on board. So I didn't eat hardtack and sow belly the rest of that trip.

I went in bathing with a number of the boys and that night woke up with a terrible burning all over my body and limbs. Mr. Houghton got some saleratus, made a strong solution with water, and washed me all over. I was covered with blotches like bee stings, but the soda relieved the burning and I was all right in the morning. They said I was poisoned with poison oak.

There were a good many sick at this time, mostly with diarrhea and typhoid fever. Mr. Houghton was taken with the typhoid. We were on duty every other day, so I did Edgar's duty one day and mine the next, so he could take care of his father in the regiment hospital. The hospital was a large wall tent near camp, with two rows of cots and room to walk between them. It was awfully hot weather, and the flies were in swarms everywhere. I think it was ten days before he was sent to St. Louis, where he died.[4]

[4] Daniel J. Houghton, Alma, Jackson County, enlisted December 17, 1861, died May 14, 1862, Jefferson Barracks, St. Louis, Missouri. Houghton, p. 40.

During this time I was on guard at the telegraph tent one night. We always had three reliefs, stood two hours on and four hours off. The sergeant called me to go on duty. I said, "Yes," but he didn't know of my faults, and I was soon snoring again. He grabbed me by the hair of the head and jerked me out of bed, which awoke the one I was sleeping with. He told the sergeant he would wake me. He did, and I went and relieved the one on post. The next morning the top of my head was awfully sore, and I was wondering what was the matter with it, when the one that woke me told me, or I would never have known.

Another night I was on a steamboat and had stood watch nearly two hours. All was quiet, and the gangplank was just high enough above the deck to sit on. I sat down and must have dropped asleep instantly. The first I knew, the sergeant touched my shoulder and said, "You are asleep."

I sprang to my feet and said, "No." The sergeant laughed.

I said, "Yes, I was asleep."

He said it was death for one to sleep while on post, but he wouldn't report it, but said some sergeants thought it cunning to do so. So I told him the circumstances, and he called the other relief and let me sleep until daylight.

Soon after Mr. Houghton was sent away, Edgar was taken with the fever, and Maxon and I took turns brushing the flies off him with a palm leaf fan. One day I got so tired, my shoulders and arms ached, and the stench from the sick was awful, and I told him I couldn't stand it any longer, but would get one of the other boys to fan him while I took a run for exercise. He didn't want anyone but me, but said I could go, but to hurry back. I was gone about an hour, but he thought I had been gone all day and told me I had ought to be ashamed. I was and didn't leave him again when I wasn't on guard, until he was sent to Evansville, Indiana.

After Corinth was taken, quite a lot of prisoners were guarded by us, and four of them enlisted in our company. One of them stayed with us three years, and was a good soldier. His story was that he had just come from Germany to New Orleans when the war broke out, was working at his trade in a tailor shop, and they discharged him for want of work, and when he applied for work they told him to enlist. So he was forced to enlist to get something to eat. Shiloh was his first battle, and he deserted the first chance he got. He served out his three years' enlistment, was wounded at Vicksburg, but came back as soon as able, was discharged at Montgomery, I think, in June, 1865, and went to New Orleans. He came down to the boat when we were on our way home and greeted us. He said he was working in the same shop he worked in before the war. That was the last I ever heard of him.[5]

We drew new tents at Pittsburg Landing, small

[5] Evidently Charles Stahl, enlisted June 15, 1862; mustered out June 14, 1865, when his term of enlistment expired. Houghton, p. 42.

wedge tents, which were more comfortable than the Sibley in warm weather. They would accommodate four men, but the regiment was so reduced by sickness there were only two in some tents.

We heard the "Dead March" now nearly every day, and I thought that the most solemn music I ever heard. It was played on muffled drum and fife. They nailed rough board boxes together to bury the dead in at this time, and carved the name, company, and regiment on a piece of board with a jackknife, or pen or pencil and stuck it at the head of the grave.

My health was good while here. I think my long rambles in the woods when not on duty helped. I also used to go to the hospital steward and get a dose of castor oil when I thought in need of it. I didn't go to the doctor while here, and but a few times the first two years.

I, with some of my company, went out in the country one day, and came to a log house that looked very old. An old man was at the gate. We asked if we could get a drink of milk. He told us to come in. It looked neat and clean. The floor was made of split logs called puncheons. A fireplace was in one end, built of stone up about five feet high, with several large, flat stones to build the fire on. The chimney was built of split sticks and mud, and plastered inside with mud. The mud was made of clay and sand. A homemade broom was at one side of the fireplace. A middle-aged woman with homespun dress dipped some milk out of an old-fashioned churn. It was buttermilk, but sweet and nice, and tasted awfully good to me. She had a gourd dipper for us to drink out of, and I drank several gourds full, and the boys called me Old Buttermilk afterwards. Some of the boys wanted sweet milk, but that was all they had as they churned the whole milk.

They were very sociable, but ignorant beyond belief. The boys had a long talk with the old man. He was "bo'n and raised in thet ere house," didn't have "nary book larnin'," didn't know what a mile was. When asked how far he had ever been from there, said he had been to Corinth two times, "reckoned" it was the farthest he had ever been. He spoke in the southern drawl that I am unable to write so you would understand it. He must have been seventy years old, but when asked said he was "right smart." He had a Negro he called his man, slept in the "loft," as he called the attic, which had a ladder on the outside and a small hole to crawl into it.

We were armed with Belgian rifles. They were heavy, but good shooting guns. At least some of them were, when carefully loaded. I saw an Indian of Company F come into camp while here with all the squirrels he could handily carry, all shot in the head. They were gray and fox squirrels. Company F was a big part Indian, and good skirmishers.

We had Enfield rifles at Vicksburg, and Springfields the last year and eight months. I liked them the best. I fetched my whole outfit home with me, gave six dollars for it. My oldest son has the gun now, the rest of the outfit has been left at different places.

We moved camp, I think in June, up to Hamburg, Tennessee,[6] some ten or twelve miles above Pittsburg Landing, where it was a healthier place and the flies were not so bad. We were the only troops there. The duty was mostly picket duty. About twenty-five were mounted for scouts, and Maxon was one of them.

One night we were on the road that went down to Pittsburg and had very strict orders, as they expected an attack of guerrillas. As soon as night came on, the sergeant posted John Preston[7] and me in an open space between the timber and the river. The bank here was two hundred feet or more above the river. There were about ten acres of thick timber between us and the road where the reserve was. We were to one sleep while the other watched. There was a good moon and not a breath of wind stirring. I stood the first part of the night and about nine o'clock I heard the picket on the road halt our scouts. Soon after a coon came out of the woods and went toward the river. I could see him plainly as he passed within a few rods of me. After that I could head twigs snap and hear the brush rattle at times, so when I woke Dixie, as we called him, I told him the woods must be full of coon as I had seen

6 Edgar P. Houghton (p. 31) says the camp was moved on July 23, 1862. E. B. Quiner uses the same date. *Military History of Wisconsin*, 602.

7 John Preston, Alma, Jackson County, enlisted December 16, 1861; mustered out October 9, 1865. Houghton, p. 41.

one and could hear them every little while. He said he would shoot them if they tried to run past him, but I didn't think he would, as our orders were to watch the river close for small boats or canoes and not to shoot until we had halted a person three times.

I lay down and went to sleep, but hadn't slept long when bang went Dixie's gun. I was wide awake, and a man down near the river was hollering, "Don't shoot. I'll surrender."

Dixie said, "Who goes there?"

"Friend, but I haven't got the countersign."

Dixie told him to come up here, and was loading his gun. The fellow kept saying, "Don't shoot." It was a citizen, who had gotten out of our guardhouse, and had been traveling in that ten acres of timber from the time our scouts came in until Dixie shot at him.

The sergeant came over to find out what we shot at and took the fellow over to the reserve. When he found out where he was, he told the sergeant he had dropped a pair of handcuffs near the river. I never knew why he was in the guardhouse, nor what became of him, but have since thought he was the same man that Reeder took the gun from across the river at Pittsburg Landing that I told of before.

One day an elderly lady and daughter came into camp horseback. (They called it critterback.) The old lady wanted to buy coffee. (The cook used to put in a good quantity of coffee without grinding to make the coffee, then spread it on the covers over the table,

Private Elisha Stockwell, Jr.

Company I, Fourteenth Wisconsin Volunteer Infantry. From
a tintype made in March, 1862, in St. Louis.

The Battle of Corinth, October 4, 1862

From a Lithograph by Currier & Ives.

dry it, and sell it to the citizens.) She wanted the green coffee, said, "Thet ere brown coffee don't 'pear to have much strength." But the cook said we didn't draw green coffee, it was all browned.

I stood close by. I had bought me a tobacco box, had it full of fine-cut, and was learning to chew. I took out my box and took a chew. The girl, about fourteen years old and handsome, neat looking, asked me for a chew. I handed her the box, and she took half there was in it and put it in her mouth. I don't know whether she thanked me or not. I was so surprised and disgusted it nearly made me sick. I spit the tobacco out of my mouth, whirled around and went to my tent, and didn't chew any more for several days. I don't know whether they bought any coffee or not. I had never seen a woman chew before that, but I learned afterwards it was quite common among the poor class to smoke and chew the same as the men. The money that the cook got for rations that he sold went into the company fund and was used to buy knicknacks for the company, such as butter, eggs, milk, or flour.

We used to draw rations of whiskey when the doctor ordered it. It was called commissary, and was dealt out to the men by the orderly sergeant, about a gill to a dose, called a jigger. One dose was enough for me. It was like drinking fire. The old topers called it A-number-one, said it was new corn whiskey and wanted age to mellow it. I and some others put ours in a bottle and used it to wash our heads with, and treat others that liked it.

One evening it was bright moonlight and cool after a hot day. We had some good singers and they sang songs and told stories, and some of us that had our bottles full let them empty them. Sergeants Crawley[8] and Higgins said we ought to have some more, and as they hadn't treated they would go and get some. There was a post sutler had his tent near our camp. They went over there. Higgins was to go to the front of the tent and engage the sutler in conversation while Crawley was to raise the back of the tent and slip out a box of wine or whiskey. Mike didn't wait until Higgins had got the sutler's attention, but grabbed the first box he got hold of and ran with it, the sutler and his Negro after him. He stubbed his toe and fell and was taken back to the tent.

Higgins wasn't so full and kept in the shade of a tree, and heard the sutler tell the Negro to go to the guardhouse and tell the officer of the guard to come up there. Higgins hurried to his tent, put on his sergeant sash and a saber he had got on the battlefield, and went to the sutler and asked what he wanted. He said, "This fellow stole a box of axes."

So Higgins took Crawley back to his tent and we all went to bed. But one went and heard the officer come to the sutler and want to know what he wanted. The next morning the sutler went to the colonel and the

---

[8] Michael Crawley, Springfield, Jackson County, enlisted November 16, 1861; made captain, December 14, 1864; mustered out October 9, 1865. Houghton, p. 39.

colonel told him to point out the man and he would punish him. So the sutler was walking through camp as he was sure he would know Crawley, as he had a good look at him. The boys were looking for him and Crawley was in his tent. One of the boys, after the sutler had walked through the camp several times told the sutler to come with him. He took him back of the cook tent and pointed to the slush hole, which was nearly full and alive with maggots. "How would you like to go in there head first?" He didn't think he would like it. Then he was told, "When you are fairly beat, you had best drop it." He dropped it. But Crawley never heard the last of the axes, and he was captain of our company when we came home. He made a good captain.

About this time I was on picket duty on a road that ran up the river and some little distance back from the river. There was a corduroy road some forty rods across what was a swampy place in a wet time, but was now dry, hard ground. I and a little French boy about my age were put on our post just after dark with orders to keep a sharp watch on the road. A little way beyond the corduroy and a few rods from the road there was some good-sized stumps about two feet high. The reserve was a short distance from the other end of the corduroy. The moon came up soon after we were out there. We were to one sleep while the other watched.

I took the first watch. About nine o'clock I heard the picket at the reserve halt the grand rounds. The night was still and the moon had got up above the trees that were on the other side of the road. I watched for the grand rounds until I thought they weren't coming to us. It must have been an hour later when I happened to look back and saw a man crawl across a strip of moonlight in the shade of those trees. He was ten rods from me. I woke the Company F boy, and told him to get behind a stump, and when I halted him, if he tried to get on his feet, we would both shoot. I was sure it was a citizen crawling up to shoot us. When I halted him, he stopped and didn't get up. So I asked him, "Who goes there?"

He said, "Grand rounds."

I said, "That's a darned pretty way to travel," then told him to advance with the countersign. He gave it and right, then began to lecture me for talking back before I got the countersign. I told him he was lucky that I didn't shoot him without halting, that I never would halt a man again that was crawling as he had done. Our orders were to halt three times before shooting. He was a captain of our regiment, and I didn't know but what I might be punished for talking as I did, but I heard no more of it.

I wanted to have said while we were at Pittsburg Landing one day, an old citizen came by our camp with two Negro women, one on either arm. They were crying as though they were heartbroken, were wiping the tears from their eyes with one hand as the man dragged them along by the other. The man was dressed in homespun and homemade clothes. His hair came to his shoulders, and whiskers covered his face and came about eight inches below his chin. He had a long, hooked nose, was leaning forward as though pulling quite a load, neither looked to the right or left, and was as unconcerned as though it was an every-day occurrence. We all looked on in silence, but my views on slavery took a change, as I had thought before that God had made the Negro for a slave for the whites.

I heard afterwards that two of our men took to the woods and overtook them, cuffed the man's ears (he was about forty years old), told him if he molested those girls again, it would go hard with him, and took the girls back to the steamboat he had taken them off of.

I heard General Halleck had given orders we mustn't harbor any runaway slaves. But Halleck left us after Corinth was evacuated and went to Washington, where he spent the rest of his valuable time. We had an elderly Negro that came to us at Pittsburg Landing and wanted to help the cook. He stayed with us until November of '62. He was a faithful fellow, honest and trustworthy. We gave him clothes and board.

I think it was in July that we left Hamburg and marched to Corinth, Mississippi, about twenty-five miles south, where we went into camp.[9] It was very hot and dusty and we were two days on the road. One man in one of the other companies got too much com-

[9] According to Quiner the regiment left Hamburg on August 23. *Military History of Wisconsin*, 602.

missary[10] and went wild. His captain tried to make him lie down and be quiet, but the more he talked to him, the noisier he got. So the captain ordered him bucked and gagged, which was done by tying his hands together and putting them down over his knees, and putting a stick over his arms and under his knees. The stick was four feet long so he couldn't roll over. They took a bayonet and tied it in his mouth with a string around his head, and he was soon as tame as a lamb.

We had all sorts of characters and one had to associate at times with all, and I think a man showed his brutal and selfish instincts more than in civil life. We had one man, whose name was Warren Foster, but all called him Mr. Foster. He was always the same to everybody. He would give his opinion when asked to, but never until asked to. He was promoted from the ranks to second lieutenant, but didn't stay long after he got his commission as his health was poor. He resigned just before the Vicksburg campaign, and I never heard of him after.[11]

Our duty at Corinth was mostly picket duty. One evening we had just got our supper, sitting in front of our tents, when the long roll was beat. We set our plates on the ground, jumped into our tents, put on our cartridge boxes and belts, grabbed our guns, got into the ranks, and counted off. Counting off was done from

10 Evidently whiskey, from what has been said above.

11 Warren Foster, Black River Falls, Jackson County, promoted for gallant conduct, October 20, 1862; resigned April 14, 1863. Houghton, p. 38.

the head of the company in the front rank by saying, "One, two, one, two." Then when the command was given, "Right face," number one in the rear rank stepped one step back and faced to the right, and number one in the front rank merely faced to the right. Numbers two stepped one on each side of number one in the rear rank, making the column four men deep. Then when ordered to front face, each number two stepped back to his place, when we were two ranks, and elbows just touched.

As soon as we had counted (this was on the company parade ground), the captain ordered, "Right face, double quick, march!" and each company was on the color line at the same time. The colonel was there and ordered, "Right face, double quick, march!" and away we went to brigade headquarters. It was just twenty minutes from the time the order to our colonel left headquarters to get his regiment there as quick as possible, until we were there. We were puffing, as it was a mile we had run. We sat down and rested, and a man from each company was sent back after our canteens.

We marched down to the depot, filled our canteens at the water tank, and as soon as it was quite dark, we took to the woods north of town. The night was dark, and for quite a way we went in single file along a cow path, but finally came out on the railroad several miles from the town, which was very small but had one big hotel called the Tishomingo Hotel. We marched all night on the railroad, and stopped at a big plantation early the next morning, and set all the Negro women to cooking hoecake, and kept them at it until the corn meal gave out. About noon an engine came down the road and knocked a two-year-old bull off the track a little way from us. Some of the boys went and skinned him, so we had some bully beef with our corn dodgers. It tasted mighty good as we hadn't eaten anything since the noon before, and the march on the railroad was awfully fatiguing. We had to step on the ties, which were a little too close together in most places for a decent step, and in places were too far apart.

As soon as it was dark, we went on down the railroad again, until about eleven o'clock, when we met a freight train which stopped, and we climbed on top and rode back to Corinth. It was said they had information that a guerrilla band intended to tear up the track and ditch a train.

We were out on three other trips of this kind, and had one man taken prisoner by the gang we were looking for. They were lying in a corn field close to the road as we passed by, and caught this fellow who had stopped beside the road. We weren't out of sight when they captured him. But they used him well and turned him over to the Rebs. They called themselves home guards. We found their headquarters in an old mill.

We drew flour while at Corinth. We had a sheet-iron oven on two wheels to bake bread for the regiment. A number of the boys had tried making bread, but some would find fault if the cook had poor luck, and the cook would quit. The oven had to be watched or it would burn the bread, or not bake fast enough. So, as no one else would do it, I took the job. I knew Bill Bradley of another company always had nice-looking bread. So I went over where he was kneading out his bread, and he told me how he made it, and I never had poor bread, and I made bread about two months.

The darky, Old Abe, did the other cooking and all I had to do was to cut the bread and see that the meals were on time, as we had to have them at a certain hour when the call was given on the drum or bugle. We had a table and benches to sit on, and a canvas over it to keep the sun and rain off. The cook was excused from guard duty, but when the regiment was called out on those raids, I had to go with them.

I had drawn a pair of new shoes when we were called out on the Iuka march. The Eighth Wisconsin was stationed at that place. The scouts told Colonel Murphy that a large body of Rebs were coming, so he started for Corinth and we met them. We struck for the north side of Iuka with our brigade, and the rest of the division went on the south side of town. We struck the road between the Reb cavalry and infantry pickets. The cavalry picket ran past us. I presume some 200 shots were fired at them, but they lay close to their horses and escaped. Presume they reported the whole Yankee army coming that way, and the whole bunch cut their way out to the south. It was said one of our regiments was badly cut up. But the Rebs got away, and we went back to Corinth at a fairly fast gait.

My shoes had pegged soles, the only ones I ever drew. They were regular old cowhides, hurt my feet, and caused a boil on the instep of my left foot. We were two days on this march as Iuka was about fifteen miles east of Corinth.[12] As I could get around camp barefoot and bake the bread, I didn't go to the doctor to get excused from duty. One day, about a week later, we got orders to be ready to march in fifteen minutes. As I couldn't wear my shoe on that foot, I went to the captain's tent and showed him my foot. He snapped me up, and said he wasn't the doctor and couldn't excuse me, which riled my temper somewhat as I knew he could and would if he hadn't been out of sorts at the time. I went and got ready and fell in with the company barefoot. The captain stood in front of the company waiting for the order to move. I was in the rear rank and Lieutenant Clancy[13] came along behind us. He was under arrest for striking an officer and couldn't go. He stopped and looked at me a moment and said, "Where are you going?"

I said, "I don't know, I am going with the company as long as I can stand it."

[12] By present-day U. S. Highway 72, Iuka is twenty-two miles from Corinth. He must have underestimated the distance.

[13] Joseph Clancy, Black River Falls, Jackson County, made second lieutenant, November 10, 1861; dismissed October 20, 1862. Houghton, p. 38.

He said in a disgusted tone, "Get out of there and take off that knapsack."

I said, "Captain Johnson says he can't excuse me."

He said, "I don't give a damn what the captain says, you get out."

I knew it was high time I was about it, and it pleased me, as the captain didn't look our way and didn't appear to hear, but marched the company off as though all was lovely.

Will say Lieutenant Clancy wasn't liked by the other officers, and a good many privates didn't like him, as there wasn't any style or military pomp about him. He was better fit for a boss in the lumber camps or log drive, and he would strike an officer as quick as a private. This was his undoing, as he was cashiered and dishonorably discharged, and went home. But years after, when he got so feeble he couldn't work, Senator Wm. T. Price got a bill through Congress removing the odium and he got a pension. He didn't have any relatives to care for him, but got a friend to care for him for his pension, and buried him after death.

He saved me from getting into a bad scrape. At that time we all thought it another wild goose chase as those trips had been before. But this one was different. The brigade went out about fifteen miles and met the Rebs under Generals Price and Van Dorn and fought them all the way back to Corinth, where the Rebs were badly defeated.[14] The next day after the regiment left, the

[14] Evidently the Battle of Corinth, October 3 and 4, 1862.

boil on the instep of my foot broke, and the next day I put my shoe on by putting my foot on the outside of the upper and tying the flaps around my ankle. I walked up the road to see how it would go that way, as it was lonesome there in the camp with the invalids. I could hear firing getting nearer all the time. I had gone about three-quarters of a mile when I met Ferdinand Yonkey[15] of my company. He wanted to know where the company was, and I told him I hadn't seen them since they left camp. He had got lost from them in falling back in the woods only a short way from where I met him, so I thought I had better get back to camp. He went back the way he had come. He told me that after he left me he didn't go but a short way when he ran into the Rebs and was captured. He was taken to Vicksburg, where he was exchanged, and got back to us in about a month.

When I got back to camp, they had everything loaded on the wagon, and we moved on to the east side of town where they were fetching the wounded. They were laying them in rows with just room to walk between. They had tents for those that were the worst off, and where they were amputating arms and legs. There was a wash-out back of one tent that had a wagon load of arms and legs. The legs had the shoes and stockings on them. In the tent where they were

[15] Ferdinand Yonkey, Lynn, Clark County, enlisted November 7, 1861; prisoner, Corinth; discharged January 3, 1863; disability. Houghton, p. 41.

coming out of the influence of the chloroform, some were groaning, some swearing, others singing.

I saw two Rebs come up to a doctor. One had all four fingers shot off one hand at about the second joint. The other was helping him along as he appeared to be weak from loss of blood. They looked like they may have been brothers. Both had their belts on. The well one held the hand while the surgeon dressed the fingers. That fellow would squat and yell every time the surgeon took up an artery, or pulled out a cord to cut it off.

The swelling had gone down in my foot so I could wear my shoe. That evening one of the boys of my company came over to the hospital to look after one of our company that was wounded, but didn't find him, so I went back with him, first taking my gun, canteen, haversack, and belts, as we thought the fight would be continued the next morning at daylight. The regiment was a little back and to the left of one of the forts of big siege guns. We didn't have any trenches for the infantry in support of the forts as they did later in the war. But the Rebs had had enough and quietly withdrew in the night.

We took their trail, and the road was lined with the dead on both sides of it, some places very thick and mostly Rebs. The Rebs dead were most of them black in the face and bloated so the buttons had burst from their clothes. Here and there would be one that was white as our dead was. It was said to have been caused by drinking whiskey with gunpowder mixed with it, and the white ones hadn't drunk the stuff.

This battle was fought the second, third, and fourth of October, 1862, I think, and that was the most horrible fifteen miles I ever marched.[16]

There were two brothers, Wils and Jack Covill.[17] Jack was a sergeant. He was wounded the third of October and died three days later. Wils with others looked for him as we marched along the road they had fought over, but they didn't find him as he had been found by others and was buried before we got back. Wils never saw him after he was wounded.

Wils was a slim, puny boy nineteen years old. I didn't think he would ever stand the hardship of a soldier's life, but he went through four years of service, is still living at the Sawtell home in Washington, and is eighty-two years old. He was a good soldier, as brave as the bravest, and as modest as a girl. I don't believe he knew what fear was. He carried the flag at Spanish Fort; and I think his brother was just as good.

When the regiment went into this battle, Dennis Murphy was color sergeant and made the remark, "I'll come out a dead sergeant or a live lieutenant." He came

16 The Confederates lost 7,000 dead and wounded and the Union Army 2,000 in this battle, according to Carl Sandburg, Abraham Lincoln: *The War Years*, (4 vols., New York, 1939), I, 598.

17 Wilson S. Covill, Irving, Jackson County, enlisted October 29, 1861, sergeant; color sergeant; mustered out October 9, 1865. Andrew J. Covill, Irving, Jackson County, sergeant; died October 6, 1862, of wounds received at Corinth, Mississippi. Houghton, pp. 38, 39.

out the live field lieutenant and a cripple for life. Although repeatedly knocked down, he hung to the flag until it was in tatters and covered with his blood.

One peculiarity of the dead was that their pants pockets were turned wrong side out. It was said to have been done by robbers of the dead. I don't remember having seen it on any other battlefield.

We were in the advance the first day, except for the cavalry, which was only a few companies. In the afternoon we heard firing ahead and soon met the cavalry coming back. The boys told them that was right, to get back out of the way so we could do the fighting. One of our boys said, "Five dollars for a dead cavalryman." Some of the cavalry smiled and took the chafing pleasantly. Others looked glum and cross. But a little way on there lay two dead cavalrymen beside the road, and I never heard that expression again. We soon came to the top of a hill overlooking a small river and open valley. Beyond in the distance we saw the Reb's train and some infantry climbing the hill some mile and a half away. Beside the road was a small cannon. It was a steel-rifled gun, called a ten-pound Rodman. It was the first time we had seen one of that make, but later learned they were a wicked little gun. I have seen them make the head logs on top of the breastworks fly a mile away.

We followed the Rebs two days and the cavalry had several skirmishes with them, but they were too few to amount to much. We marched back to Corinth in a cold, drizzly rain, and as I didn't have my blankets, I was wet through. I suffered that night as we had only green wood to make a fire. It stopped raining so I got my clothes partly dried. I lay down on the wet ground to sleep, but would get so cold that I would have to get up and hover over the smoky fire. I put in about the most disagreeable night of my life, and was nearly sick when we got back to camp.

I hadn't been to the doctor up to this time, and thought I would be all right in a few days. But we had dress parade a few days later and I fainted away. They carried me to my tent, and when I came to, I was shaking with the ague—they call it malaria fever nowadays. As long as I was in the army and nearly a year after I got home, I had it every time I caught cold. I would break it up with quinine and Dover's powders. I was all right in a few days.

About this time Ed Houghton got back from the hospital. His hair had all fallen out, but otherwise he was looking fine and wasn't sick again to speak of while in the service. Maxon had been discharged in September.

We were out on one of those raids one time, I don't remember whether before or after the battle. It was hot and very dusty and all the water we could get was out of the wells along the road. They were quite a way apart. As we came in sight of one house, the regiment ahead was leaving the well, which was some rods in front of the house and near the road. We saw a woman run out to the well and cut the rope, letting both buckets fall in the well. The water was pulled up over a pulley; one bucket going down as the other came up. We marched a little past the house and stopped and sat down. The colonel sent his orderly back with four men and burned the house. They didn't let the woman take anything out—only what she had on. This looked tough to me, but it was war and it was a good lesson to her at least, and possibly to others.

CHAPTER III

VICKSBURG AND A FURLOUGH

I think we left Corinth about the last of November or fore part of December on what was called the Holly Springs march. The boys that had been taken prisoner at Corinth were marched over this same road by the Rebs to Vicksburg, had been exchanged, and were again with us. They had been ill treated by the citizens. There was lots of foraging on this march and houses burned. The fences on both sides of the road, which were what was called worm fences, built of oak rails, were on fire in places. The smoke was stifling. This was said to have been done by men that had been prisoners. In one case a woman had spit in one boy's face while stopped to rest and being exhibited by their captors to the citizens along the road.

But this time, they were all good Union people, so there were very strict orders against foraging and also against straggling. We had roll call every time we halted, and if one missed roll call and couldn't give a good excuse, he was punished. I don't remember all the different fines, but our cartridge box was inspected three times a day, and if a cartridge was missing, it was fifty cents, and ten dollars for killing a hog, to be taken out of the next payroll. But we had fresh meat when in real need, and the officers would look the other way when they heard a hog squeal, if the men were decent about it. So the boys were careful about straggling or foraging. I never heard of but one that was fined, which I will speak of later.

I think it was the third day on this march, a long train was ahead, and we stopped quite often. Water was scarce, the houses way back from the road, and our canteens all dry. The day was hot and dusty. About the middle of the afternoon we saw a small creek about fifty rods from the road. Ed Houghton said he would take the canteens of the company and go fill them if I would take his gun if they moved along before he got back. Before he got back, we started, and didn't stop until way after dark. I carried his gun, and this was the time I spoke of before—there were only four privates to stack arms when we stopped. Ed carried the canteens full of water until he was nearly tired out, then emptied the water out and carried them into camp. They were a good load empty.

We stopped here several days, near Grand Junction, Mississippi. We had division drill one day, the only time I remember of so many troops on drill. It was a grand sight that one had to see to appreciate.

Ed was detailed to guard the teams on a foraging trip to get feed for the mules. He saw the wagon master put a big sweet potato in one of the wagons, and on the way back he got that potato. It was so long he couldn't hide it in his haversack, so he put the haversack on under his coat, and in camp asked me if I could hide it. I said yes, made a hole in the middle of the fire and covered it with ashes and coals, and we waited till all had laid down. (We had a tent by ourselves.) When we dug it out, it was baked fine and we had all we could eat that night and the next morning. That was the best as well as the biggest potato I ever saw. No doubt the wagon master used some bad language, but we thought we had as good a right to it as he did, and he had a better chance to forage than we did.

We had both been brought up not to steal or lie and I despise a thief or liar now. When we foraged, though, we thought of it as a part of war and punishment of the enemy.

There was a large plantation house near our camp, and the officers got a young lady to sing and play on the piano. The window was open, and us soldiers were outside and heard the singing, which was good. She was good looking, had a good voice, and sat near the window. This was the first piano I had ever heard played. She sang "The Bonny Blue Flag," one stanza:

> *We are a band of brothers*
> *And natives of the soil*
> *A-fighting for our property*
> *We gained by honest toil.*

It impressed me very much, and I thought they might be in the right, but one of the officers sang:

Vicksburg and a Furlough

The Star Spangled Banner
Oh long may she wave
O'er the land of the free
And the home of the brave.

He was a good singer and gave as good as she sent. She was a good sport and took it pleasantly, she singing one song and he the next. I don't think I ever heard a concert I enjoyed more.

I had never thought of politics, thought it only for old men to quarrel over. But I began to form my views of politics before I knew it.

There were three classes of whites and two of Negroes. The Negroes were the servants—I should say, body and house servants, and those called the field hands, just niggers. The white people were gentlemen, quality folks, and po' white trash. I heard a southerner say a nigger was worth one thousand dollars while a poor white man wasn't worth anything. This helped to change my views of slavery. But I must cut out my thoughts and try to stick more closely to my experience.

We marched from here one day's march south of Holly Springs, where we lay two or three days. While there I went out with George Reeder to get some fresh meat. I had a navy revolver and Reeder had a small revolver he borrowed from one of the boys. It shot ten times out of five barrels in the cylinder, all muzzle loaded.

We had to steal through the picket line which was

in the woods. Out about one and a half miles from the pickets we came to a house. Near the house were some hogs, old sows and rather poor, but we thought they would do. As it was a drizzly, rainy day, I had my revolver under my coat. Reeder got in the pen and began to shoot at the hogs. A man came out and said those were his brood sows, and if we must have some pork, to take one of the shoats he had in a pasture near by, and he would help get one. So Reeder told him we would just as soon take one of the shoats. The fellow got a good club and went with us. But before we got the pigs up to the corner of the pasture, I noticed he was following Reeder close behind, and saw him look up at Reeder's head. He had his club in both hands as if to stroke. I gave Reeder a nod and he looked behind him. Reeder told him to get from behind him if he was going to help us get a pig, and I pulled my revolver out so he could see I had a gun. He threw down his club and went to the house.

Reeder shot several times before he would give up. That gun wouldn't kill a hog, and the pigs got so wild we couldn't get near them. Then I got in some brush near one corner of the pasture and Reeder drove them into the corner, but they went over the fence like a flock of sheep into the woods. Then Reeder wanted to go back to the house and take one of the sows, but I told him I was going to camp as that man might get some neighbors or there might be some Reb cavalry close by. So we went to camp without any meat, and I wouldn't go with him any more.

We heard afterwards there was Reb cavalry not far off. They took Holly Springs a few days later, burned Grant's depot of supplies, and changed his plans to take Vicksburg by that way.

We were two days' march south of Holly Springs when it was burned, and marched back in one day. But the Rebs had gone. Colonel Murphy was in command there. He was colonel of the Eighth Wisconsin, had two pieces of artillery, and two companies of the Second Illinois Cavalry that were camped just outside the village. There was also a regiment of engineers about a mile distant guarding a railroad bridge. They had fortified themselves. Murphy surrendered without firing a gun, but the cavalry and engineers didn't surrender, and the Rebs left them alone, but paroled the Eighth and left. I understood Colonel Murphy was dishonorably discharged for this.

We marched back near Grand Junction and laid in camp here several days. I was on picket duty one day, posted on the turnpike going west toward Memphis, Tennessee, with heavy timber on both sides. There came an old sow and a nice litter of pigs. I and one of the other boys got clubs and got two nice pigs that weighed about thirty pounds apiece. We skinned them, and that was as nice meat as I ever ate. The hogs ran wild in the woods at this time and lived on nuts, of which there was an abundance this year. The meat had a nutty flavor. It tasted more like bear meat than pork.

Two of the boys got some goats, with the only goat milk I ever tasted. After frying the meat, we fried our hardtack in the gravy, as we had a frying pan, and we had supper fit for a king, with milk in our coffee. There were four of us.

I came on post near midnight one night. There was a full moon, not a cloud, nor a breath of air stirring, and so quiet—only the night birds. My post was beside a large tree on the south side of the pike, in the shade of the trees. The reserve was back out of sight of the road, where there was a good fire, as the night was quite cold. I was all alone with my thoughts when I saw someone coming on the run quite a way off. He was in the shade, clear to one side of the road, which was covered with grass.

I couldn't hear his footsteps, and my hearing and eyes were good. It was a mystery to me how he could glide along so still. I stepped behind the tree, cocked my gun, and let him come so close that I felt sure I could hit him if he tried to get away. When I halted him and asked, who goes there, he replied, "Friend without countersign."

I told him to advance. When within eight feet, I told him to halt. The sergeant had heard me challenge him and came and questioned him. This was his story. The Rebs had captured him that day as he was out foraging. They told him they would shoot him at sunrise the next morning. He pulled off his boots, coat, and hat, lay down with his blanket over him, and pretended to sleep as a guard was placed over him. He watched the guard who sat near him with his gun across his lap. When the guard began to nod his head and finally dropped his head to his breast and slept, he slid out from under his blanket and crawled some distance on his hands and knees. Then he got to his feet and ran for dear life until out of breath, then got into a thicket until he got his breath, then cut and ran. He had run three times in this way when he came to the road a short distance before I halted him.

When I halted him, he thought he had run onto a Reb picket, but was so close he didn't think he could get away. He was bare headed and barefoot, and was a tickled man when we told him we were the Four-teenth Wisconsin. He belonged to the Kansas Jay-hawkers, and his regiment was camped near ours. The sergeant took him to the reserve, and gave him roast pig, hardtack, and coffee, as the Rebs hadn't given him any supper. He then rolled up in a blanket and slept till breakfast. The next morning he was sent to his regi ment with a guard, and I never heard of him after.

One day we were marching along a road, and the Negroes would come running to the road to see the "Massa Lincum" soldiers. They were dressed in their Sunday's best, and were as tickled as mortals could be. There was a white lady with them at one place where we halted. She was of the quality class and appeared to be as pleased as the darkies were. She said in the southern drawl, "My, you'uns look jes like we'uns. They tole we'uns that you'uns had horns." One of the boys said, "We have, but we never show our horns to the ladies." I presume this was the first Yanks she had seen. I can't make you understand just how comical they appeared. They thought the whole Yankee army was there.

We marched from here to Memphis, Tennessee, where we camped about two miles outside the city. We hadn't been paid off during the last six months, and lots of the men were dissatisfied. There was said to be a place down in the city where they would give a soldier a suit of citizen's clothes and one hundred dollars in money to desert. Quite a few took this chance to go home, but President Lincoln issued a proclamation that all who returned to their commands within thirty days would be pardoned. Nearly all came back. There was only one who deserted from our company. That was Curly that boxed my ears at Fond du Lac, and he never returned.[1]

There was lots of stealing here out of the stores by our division, so much that the stores closed their doors. This was because we thought it a Rebel stronghold.

We were paid two months' pay and boarded the boats for down the river toward Vicksburg. We went to Lake Providence, where they had dug a canal from the river into the lake, which was about one mile wide and two long, running back from the river. We lay here I think a month.

[1] Edgar P. Houghton (p. 45) reports 5 deserters among the 161 enlisted men in the company.

Vicksburg and a Furlough

We went on one march to guard the engineers who were sent to look over a contemplated canal from the lake to Bayou Macon. It was swamp all the way—about fifteen miles. There was quite a stream of water ran through the swamp so the engineers went with a canoe, and we waded through the jungle. In places, where the water was too deep to wade, we had to fell trees to get across. We were two days on this trip. When I got back, my pants were gone up to my crotch, but I had a good pair of cotton flannel drawers on, or the hide would have been torn from my legs by the briars and canebrake. A number in the regiment were in the same fix as I, so I went to the doctor for the first time and got excused from duty until I could draw some pants.

We went from here to some ten miles above Vicksburg, where we lay until we started on the Vicksburg campaign about the first of April, 1863.

We marched across the country west of the Mississippi River to Grand Gulf below Vicksburg, where we crossed the river on transports that had run past Vicksburg. The boat showed the marks of the shot that had been fired at it. From here we marched to the rear of Vicksburg.

We were under the same orders against foraging. One evening we went into camp before dark. It had drizzled rain and we were tired and hungry. We stacked arms, and the orders against foraging were read. The colonel said, "Boys, you have heard the orders. Now I don't want to see a d——d man touch any of them sheep we just passed, and these hogs, I don't want to see anyone touch them. Break ranks!" The boys caught their guns with bayonets on and took after the hogs. They would surround and kill them with the bayonet. Reeder ran past the colonel who was going for his tent. He said, "Reeder, don't shoot."

When Reeder shot the hog, headquarters was in sight not far off, and orders were read next morning fining Reeder ten dollars for killing that hog. Reeder was mad because no one else was fined. He thought the colonel used partiality. But when told that the colonel had told him not to shoot, he said he wouldn't chase the hog for ten dollars anyway.

A few days later we were rear guards when the Battle of Champion Hills was fought. We were stopped at Raymond to protect the hospital where the wounded were being cared for. We were out of rations and the train of wagons was ahead of us. Reeder and some others went out and got two of the nicest hogs I saw in the South. They were skinning them when the colonel came along. Reeder said, "Hello, Colonel, what are hogs worth tonight?"

The colonel said, "Not much, pretty poor meat, ain't it?" Reeder took a nice ham over to the colonel's cook that night.

The next morning we crossed the battlefield—where the dead lay thick—both the Blue and the Gray. This was a severe battle for the number engaged.

We followed the Rebs into Vicksburg and commenced the siege of that place the eighteenth day of May, 1863. It lasted until July 4.

The twenty-second of June the regiment charged the Rebs' fortifications, but were badly repulsed, losing nearly one-half of its number in killed and wounded in about ten minutes.[2] After this we dug up to them. It was two rods from the outside of our fort to the outside of the Rebs' fort. Moonlight nights they used to agree to have a talk, and both sides would get up on the breastworks and blackguard each other and laugh and sing songs for an hour at a time, then get down and commence shooting again.

Finally some of each side met halfway between the lines and traded tobacco for hardtack. One night some of the Rebs came over to our side, where the Eleventh Illinois boys were, and had coffee. When two brothers met and the one in the Eleventh asked his brother if he was going back, he said he was. But his brother told him he never would live to get back if he started. So he concluded to stay on our side. This stopped the armistice and fun they had been having.

We had the Rebs undermined and the powder ready

[2] Edgar P. Houghton (p. 33) reports, "The Fourteenth went into the Vicksburg campaign about two hundred and fifty strong and lost in killed, wounded, and missing, one hundred and seven men."

Quiner says of the Fourteenth Regiment on this occasion: "In the terrible charge of the 22nd, the Fourteenth took a conspicuous part, penetrating a considerable distance beyond any other regiment of the brigade, and attaining a position in front of the enemy's fort, where no other regiment was near them. Here they were obliged to seek cover until night approached before they could escape." *Military History of Wisconsin*, 605–606.

to put in. It was camp talk that we would blow up their forts the Fourth of July, and make a general charge. But they put up the white flag the third, and marched outside their works the morning of the Fourth. Our regiment was one of the regiments that went in and took possession.[3] But we marched back to our camp that night and lay there until the Rebs had been paroled and marched out.

Soon after the surrender, we went by steamboat to Natchez, Mississippi,[4] and took possession of that city. We were provost guards there and camped in the court-house square a big part of the summer.[5] This was a nice city and we had a nice time there.

We used to two go together when on patrol. One day I was with a boy about my age that belonged to another company. He had found where he could sell Confederate money for ten cents on the dollar, and we could buy it for from three cents to five cents. We made forty dollars that day. But we bought some of a Thirty-third Wisconsin boy that was printed on white paper. It was just imitation of Rebs' money, but wasn't signed.

[3] Edgar P. Houghton (p. 33) puts it as follows. "On the fourth of July, '63, the Fourteenth was assigned the position of honor on the right and ordered by General Ransom to take the advance in the triumphal march of our troops into the city."

Quiner adds that General Ransom complimented the regiment with the remark that "every man and officer of the Fourteenth was a hero." *Military History of Wisconsin*, 606.

[4] July 12, 1863. Houghton, p. 33; Quiner, *Military History of Wisconsin*, 606.

[5] Until October 9, 1863. Houghton, p. 33.

We colored the paper with coffee and got Nate Clapp of my company, who was a good penman, to sign it. We had a genuine bill for a sample, and it passed all right. But the Reb citizen we sold it to found out it was counterfeit, and wouldn't buy any more from the Yanks. So we ruined our business by being dishonest.

There were about thirty of us mounted for scouts. We were quartered in what had been a livery barn, and one evening I was in charge when a citizen came with an order from the provost marshal to take care of his horse. So I took his horse in and fed it. In talking, he asked me where I was from. I told him, and he asked me if I knew George Reeder. When I told him I did, he said, "That is my boy."

But I had heard Reeder say his father had died some years before the war in New Orleans. The old man got more excited the more I told him. They were father and son, both thinking the other dead. The old man had come in to get some arms and ammunition to protect himself against the Rebs, but they furnished him transportation up to Illinois and I never knew what became of him. But his son was wounded at Shiloh in the hip, and that leg was shorter than the other. The old fellow had one leg shorter too, so both walked with the same hitch to their walk.

George Reeder died in the Soldiers' Home at Milwaukee some years after the war. He could have had his discharge at Shiloh, but wouldn't take it. I often came on duty with him, and so was forced in his company. He had some serious faults, but was generous, and I believe honest, fearless, and truthful.

From here we went back to Vicksburg, where we did picket duty. (I didn't tell much about the siege of Vicksburg, so will tell it here as some of it may interest you.) On the nineteenth of May we pushed the Rebs back to their breastworks, which was about three miles back from the river on a steep ridge and quite high. The timber had been stashed down in front. We had two men wounded in my company. One had his ear pierced in the lower part with a small bullet or buckshot.[6] The other was hit on the shin by a spent ball which didn't go through his pants.[7] But he thought it had gone through his leg, and it made him lame for several days.

We were under fire here forty-seven days. Our camp was in a ravine where not many bullets got in, but often went overhead with a nasty whine. One night four of us had an oilcloth spread on the ground and were playing poker when we heard a bullet whine. It came straight down through the middle of the oilcloth, but we kept on playing.

We were on duty every other day, either digging trenches or sharpshooting. We used to dig trenches days and nights when the moon shone, until they surrendered. When sharpshooting, we would shoot at them

[6] Evidently Charles F. Bone, according to Houghton (p. 32).
[7] N. M. Clapp. Houghton, p. 32.

66

where they went over a hill nearly a mile away, and by putting in two charges of powder, we could make them get over that hill on the double quick.

After the surrender, I was on picket duty one day, and Reeder and I picked up lead and run it in bars. We sold it to a sutler, I think for four cents a pound. We got four dollars apiece. It was said that the soldiers dug the breastworks all over for the lead after we left.

There was a large cemetery near the picket line which showed the effects of the siege. One vault had the door wrecked, but the coffins were unhurt. They were metallic with glass tops. In one was a man who had been killed in a duel several years before. He was shot in the forehead with a large ball. It looked like beads of sweat on his face. In another was the bones of a little child. These were all I looked at.

We re-enlisted here in the latter part of December, 1863, for three years or during the war. But as I hadn't been in two years, I couldn't re-enlist until my two years were up. But I promised to re-enlist. We were to get $300 and a thirty-day furlough, so I went home with the regiment.[8] The furlough was the big inducement.

8 This was when the Fourteenth Wisconsin became a "veteran" regiment, adding that designation to its title. Edgar Houghton has clearly explained the procedure for earning the designation in the following words. At Vicksburg, "on December 11 the regiment became a veteran regiment. A regiment, in order to become a veteran regiment, must have served two years of the three for which they enlisted; then if two-thirds or more of the regiment will re-enlist they have the privilege of returning to the state as a regiment, where

We went up the river in January, 1864, to Cairo, Illinois, thence by rail to Madison, Wisconsin, where we were paid two months' pay and got our furlough. The two months' pay was $26 and we had to pay our fare from there home.

We paid the conductor instead of buying a ticket, and the conductor gave me a bad one-dollar bill in change. It was quite dark and I didn't look at it, but put it in my vest pocket. Soon they lit the lights and the train peddler came along with some apples, and I out with the bill to buy some apples. He said, "That ain't money." It was an old state bank bill called "wildcat money" before the war. So when the conductor came along I told him how I knew he gave it to me. But he wouldn't make it right. So I told him if he made anything out of it to let me know. I had paid to Sparta. I had intended to go home first and then to La Crosse to see my sister. So I thought I would go to La Crosse first and get even with that conductor.

After we passed Sparta, he wanted my fare, which was ninety cents.

---

they receive a furlough of thirty days. The men re-enlisting are mustered out and mustered in again for three years, receiving three hundred and two dollars bounty in addition to the one hundred dollars for the first enlistment."

Twenty-five of the original eighty-eight who comprised Company I on March 8, 1862, that being all who were with the regiment at the time, re-enlisted at this time and were therefore veterans. Houghton, pp. 34, 44.

Quiner says that the Fourteenth Wisconsin Volunteer Regiment was the first regiment in the Army of the Tennessee to re-enlist. *Military History of Wisconsin*, 607.

I handed out the bad one-dollar bill, but he said he wouldn't take it. I told him, "You won't take anything then." He told me to get off at the next station, but when by that station he said, "I told you to get off."

I said, "I did get off and you hollered 'All aboard,' and I got on again."

He reached for the bell cord and said, "I'll put you off here."

I said, "You haven't men enough to put me off."

The car was full of Company D of my regiment, and they hollered, "Put *him* off." So I told him we were just about even, and he went on, but would look daggers at me every time he came by.

My brother-in-law kept a hotel and had a barroom. He was a Frenchman. One day I was sitting by the stove when another man came in. He was talking French with Nick,[9] which I didn't understand, and he finally came and sat by me. He asked me if I knew what I was fighting for. I told him that I didn't care to talk politics— wasn't posted in that line. He told me how the South was being abused, that we never could whip them, and finally said he would bet I couldn't tell him what I was fighting for. I told him I was fighting to whip just such men as he was, and I would think more of him if he would take a gun and go down there and help them. He got disgusted with me and said I was too ignorant for him to talk to. Nick laughed at him and he went out. I suspected Nick was one of a gang who were trying

[9] Nick Jarvis, La Crosse, Wisconsin, Stockwell's brother-in-law.

to induce soldiers to desert and go to Canada, and told my sister as much. But they let me alone after that.

I went up home from here. Then I got an order to report to Milwaukee at once. My furlough wasn't half out, but four of us went to Milwaukee, and there I met my future wife.[10] I took the rest of my furlough there and got it extended twice by the provost marshal. I could have gotten a detail for his office boy, but wouldn't take it. I got married, and soon went south.

There were three of us on this trip, Lieutenant Manley,[11] George Dunn,[12] and myself. When we got on the steamboat at Cairo, Illinois, they took all three of us for officers and gave us staterooms, and we got our meals in the cabin all the way down to Vicksburg.

[10] Katherine Hurley of Milwaukee, Wisconsin. They were married March 14, 1864, and lived together nearly sixty-three years.

[11] Andrew J. Manley, Neillsville, Clark County, mustered in October 19, 1861; sergeant; first sergeant; first lieutenant, September 2, 1862; mustered out, May 22, 1865. Houghton, p. 38.

[12] George W. Dunn, Alma, Jackson County, enlisted February 9, 1864; mustered out October 9, 1865. Houghton, p. 42.

CHAPTER IV

TO ATLANTA WITH GENERAL SHERMAN

At Vicksburg we found about one-half of the regiment. The other half had gone with General Banks up the Red River and had left no communication. So we were detached and went to Sherman, and were called Major Worden's battalion.[1] We took a steamer up to Cairo, Illinois, then up the Ohio River to the Cumberland River, up that river quite a way, got off at a very small place and marched across the country to the Tennessee River. We crossed that river on a pontoon bridge near Huntsville, Alabama. I think that was the name of the place.

We lay there one day while they were laying the

[1] The battalion was composed of detachments of the Fourteenth Wisconsin and Eighty-first and Ninety-fifth Illinois, under the command of Major Asa Worden. Robert U. Johnson and Clarence C. Buell (eds.), *Battles and Leaders of The Civil War* (4 vols., New York, 1887), IV, 288.

Edward P. Houghton indicates that he and Stockwell were separated at this time, he being with that part of the regiment which went west with General Banks. He records in some detail the experience of Company I personnel with the Sixteenth Corps in the West. Houghton, pp. 35–36.

According to Quiner no report was made to the Adjutant General of the operations of Worden's battalion during the Atlanta campaign and therefore he was unable to find any account of its activities. *Military History of Wisconsin*, 609.

bridge. There was the largest spring near where we camped. It was twelve or fourteen feet across, and two or three feet deep. It was clear as crystal, and the water bubbled the white sand up all over the bottom. A small mill was a few rods below for grinding corn. It was run by the water from the spring.

This was a long, hard march, especially hard on the recruits. There was quite a number of them. They cut their blankets up and tied them on their blistered feet and carried their shoes hung on their guns. Forage was very scarce as both armies had been over this country during the last two years.

We halted one day in front of a large house. The man was leaning on the fence talking with the boys when a long-legged rooster came between the house and road with two soldiers after him. If ever a rooster ran, that one was doing it. The boys hollered, "Go! Go!" and all laughed. The man seemed to enjoy the race as well as the rest of us. They were soon out of sight in the shrubbery.

I said to the man, "It is tough to have men chase your chicks in your dooryard."

He said, "I expected that when the war broke out. You fellows have got to have something to eat. That rooster is the last living thing on this place, and if they can catch him they are welcome to it." But the Rebs got the most of them. He didn't claim to be Union or Reb, but I believe he was Union. He was at least a sensible, pleasant man.

After crossing the Tennessee River, we marched over a spur of Lookout Mountain, which took two days. We didn't get any water from morning until night each day, and our canteens held about three pints.

We stopped next at Athens, Alabama, a small village on the railroad where they looked for the Reb cavalry to strike the railroad. We were here several days. We would form line of battle before daylight each morning and wait for the Rebs that never came.

The cows from the town ran along a small creek a little way from camp. Farrand Baker[2] of my company had a felon on his left thumb. The doctor had lanced it and it was getting well. He said, "Let's go and see if we can get some milk." So we took a canteen and went over to the creek which was lined on both sides with willows. We tried several cows that were gentle, but they had evidently just been milked. There was an old brindle cow that looked as if she hadn't been milked, but she wouldn't let us get near her. So I hid in a bunch of willows where there was a path, Baker drove her through, and I grabbed her by the horns. She took me out into an open spot, and I got her by the nose with one hand. She finally gave up, and Baker milked her with his well hand and held the canteen with the other. He had the canteen nearly full when the cow kicked the canteen about sixteen feet into the brush and hit Baker's thumb. I let the cow go and ran to save the milk

[2] Farrand Baker, Melrose, Jackson County, enlisted October 21, 1861; sergeant; mustered out October 9, 1865. Houghton, p. 39.

which I could hear "gurgle, gurgle," but the last drop had run out before I found the canteen. It had caught in the brush upside down. Baker was jumping around hanging onto his thumb, and calling that cow all sorts of names. But she didn't stop to hear, and we went back to camp without any milk.

The next morning after it began to get light, Charley King[3] and I went over to town, which was about eighty rods. The first cow yard we came to had two cows in it. They were gentle, and I soon filled my canteen. I was waiting for King to fill his when I saw the old man come out of the house. We got out of there, had gotten ten or twelve rods when he hollered, "Fetch that milk back."

King asked him who he was talking to.

He said, "You uns."

King said, "It is a pretty idea when we can't walk along the street with water without you hollering at us to fetch milk back."

So he started for the cow yard and we went to camp and had milk in our coffee that morning. My, how good it tasted! But we left enough so he could have milk in his coffee too.

I was on picket duty one night while here, about three-quarters of a mile from camp. I was acting corporal and had two Company F Indians. One, a recruit, couldn't talk or understand our language, and the other

[3] Charles H. King, Hixton, Jackson County, enlisted February 19, 1864; mustered out October 9, 1865. Houghton, p. 43.

had to give him his orders. He was posted in front and across the road from the house. When I went to relieve him, he was gone and I had to go and get the other one to find him. He had gone down the road some forty rods to the woods, where he could get out of sight, as it was open ground where I had posted him. The Indians were good skirmishers, but didn't like the open country or pitched battle.

After leaving Athens, we camped one night near Cave Spring. There was a large creek came out of a mountain here. Four of us crawled into the cave a little way from where the creek came out. After we got in, we lit a candle and went in near thirty rods. It was like great cracks in the solid rock. I think it was limestone. In places there were rooms ten feet wide and several rods long, and overhead were what looked like great icicles hanging down from the ceiling, which was ten feet or more high. There were great cracks and fissures leading off, some wide enough for two to walk abreast, and some just wide enough for one to squeeze through. We finally came to where it was straight down, and we could hear the water running over quite a falls. By dropping a stone, we judged it was fifteen or twenty feet down to the water. The citizens said that one could go in half a mile or more, but one could get lost in there. I believed it, and I saw all I wanted of it.

The icicles were formed by the water dripping down. They glistened in the candlelight. The chasm where we dropped stones was so wide we couldn't throw a stone across it. The echo of our voices came back to us. The water was clear and cold.

One day I was on rear guard. When they halted and I went up to the regiment, I noticed one of the recruits, Adam Relyea,[4] didn't feel well. As I had my knapsack carried on the wagon, I took his and put it with mine, and the next halt went up and got his gun. He never forgot the little kindness. The next day he had to ride in the ambulance as he was down with typhoid fever. It was hot and dusty and he wanted me to wash and care for him, although there were two men that came from the same place, and he and I were strangers. I went and cared for him while we were in camp, and we were fast friends after as long as he lived. He died April 11, 1915, and I went nearly one thousand miles to attend his funeral. He rode in the ambulance two days until we got to Rome, Georgia, where he was left in the hospital. He came back to us soon after Atlanta was taken.

On the march from Rome to Kingston, we were rear guards, and it was long after dark when the regiment got to camp. It was long after dark before the moon came up, and I was very tired. When they began going into camp ahead, we on the rear would drag along, sometimes going only a few rods between stops. It was woods on both sides of the road, and I would drop my knapsack on the ground and sit down on it. I was

4 Adam L. Relyea, Springfield, Jackson County, enlisted January 13, 1864; corporal; mustered out October 9, 1865. Houghton, p. 43.

on the left hand side of the road the last I remembered. When I awoke, the moon was some two hours high and I sat facing the road. All was still. I had to do some thinking before I made out just where I was, and how I came to be there. But I soon knew what had happened, and I thought I could hear some one snoring in the direction I should go. A little back from the road were two men covered up with their blankets. I didn't disturb them but took the road. I was so cold and refreshed, I took a lively run to warm up. I must have gone two miles or more when I met an empty mule train. I passed two or three teams when I asked how far it was to Kingston. The driver said, "If you are going to Kingston get in and ride, that is where we are going." So I got in and rode. I don't know how I got turned around unless I must have gotten up in my sleep and gone some distance and sat down on the opposite side of the road at the next stop. I don't know how far I would have gone if I hadn't met those teams.

We soon got to Kingston, and there were campfires in every direction. As I had no idea where to look for my regiment, I lay down near the road and slept the sweet sleep of youth until daylight. The next morning I went on to the farthest side of the camp and sat down beside the road until my regiment came along, when I was once more at home in Dixie Land, and had once more escaped serious consequences of my sleepiness. One of the boys had drawn my rations and fetched them along for me.

The next day, I think it was, I was on rear guard and the sergeant sent me to a house to see if there were any soldiers there. I found one in the kitchen up on a chair looking on the top of a cupboard for plunder. I made that fellow get out of there mighty lively. There was a woman on a bed in one corner of the room crying and sobbing. Another woman sat on a chair near the bed and looked daggers at me or the other fellow, but didn't say a word. I had my bayonet to the seat of that fellow's pants and told him to get a move on. He was running as far as I could see him. This was the only pillaging I ever saw while in the army, and I will say I had no time for that sort of business, and I never went into a house unless ordered to.

I had an aunt that lived about thirty miles from Atlanta at Villa Rica, Georgia. She was my mother's sister, and I thought as much of her as I did of my mother. I didn't know at that time just where they lived so was looking for her every time I saw a lady, as I knew she lived near Atlanta.

We came to Sherman at Big Shanty near Kennesaw Mountain, and took position on the left of the mountain. I had a bad boil under my right arm, and went to the doctor, but he didn't excuse me from duty. He told me to come and have it lanced when I thought it ready to open. In about an hour we were ordered to fall in, and we advanced on a spur of the mountain, which was nearly a mile from us. The Rebs were throwing shells at us from the top of the hill which was covered with brush nearly as high as our heads. It was quite steep, so when we got to the foot of the hill, we were out of sight of the Rebs. We expected to catch a shower of bullets when we reached the top, but they were gone when we got up there.

I broke the boil though before I got halfway up the hill. But it began to gather again the next day, and the doctor went to scolding because I didn't come and have it lanced. I told him I broke it climbing the hill. So he said, "When it gets ready to open again, come and have it lanced." But the next day I was detailed to work on the breastworks, and I broke it shoveling. This time I got one of the boys to squeeze it out, and it got well. But this put me against the old doctor, so I didn't go to him for some time.

I knew I ought to have some physic, but put it off until one day we went on the extreme left to make a feint on the Rebs' right. We marched several miles and drove in their pickets, which were nearly a mile in front of their breastworks, and saw a Reb that one of the Company F Indians had taken prisoner. He was the most disgusted Reb I ever saw. He was behind some rails they had piled up to protect them, and out in front was an open field with big stones, some higher than a man, and near the woods, which were big trees and no underbrush. He said he saw the Indian go behind the stone, and was waiting for him to come out to get a shot at him, when the first thing he knew the Indian's gun came over the end of the rails and there was nothing to do but surrender. He asked the Indian if he was the one that went behind the stone. The Indian said he was, but wouldn't tell the Reb how he got out without being seen. The Reb said he had read of the Indians doing such things, but didn't believe such yarns, but had to believe it this time. He said he didn't care so much about being taken prisoner, but hated to have such a game as that played on him. The Indian just laughed at him as did the rest of us.

We soon came in sight of their breastworks with an open field in front, and two forts that commanded it some fifty or sixty rods from us, when the color bearer heard someone order, "Halt!" He lay down as all the rest of us did. The forts opened fire at the same time with grape and canister, which were a little far off to be effective. Next came the shells. We were too close for them as they went over us and didn't burst until they had passed. But the Seventeenth Wisconsin was just over the ridge, which was covered with timber, and they had a number killed that I saw when we fell back. I never heard how many were lost, but we only had one wounded. We lay there nearly an hour with those shells flying over us. We were sent there to hold the Rebs so they couldn't reinforce their left where our men charged, but were repulsed.

When I got back, I was nearly played out as my bowels hadn't moved the last five days. I went to the doctor again, and he gave me a big dose of salts, but they didn't operate. I went back the next morning and

he gave me the same dose. I asked the steward if he
didn't have some castor oil. He said he could give only
what the prescription called for. So I went back to
the doctor and asked him if I couldn't have some oil
as I didn't like the salts. He snapped me up, and said
I could take such medicine as he gave me. I told him
I could, but darned if I would. He said, "Don't be
saucy." Then I began to tell him what I thought of him,
but the sergeant took me by the collar, led me away,
and told me I would get into trouble. So I went to my
tent, and the lieutenant came and talked to me, told
me not to go to that doctor any more, and said he would
give me an order to go to the Seventeenth Wisconsin
doctor. I said I wouldn't go to any doctor, nor take
any doctor's medicine, nor do duty until able, and didn't
ask any favors from him or anyone else. He laughed at
me and said I was mighty important, but when I felt
able to, to report to the sergeant for duty. The next
day I didn't need any physic, and think if I had taken
that other dose it would have killed me. I had a run
of chronic diarrhea, and got so weak I could hardly
walk.

The lieutenant came one day and said I would have
to go to the hospital. I said I wouldn't go.

He said, "Don't get funny. I have orders to send all
who are not able to march back to the hospital, and
you are going. I have enough men to take you there."

I said, "Yes, I'll go," and there was another man
from one of the other companies that went with me.

It was about one mile to the rear. When we got back there, we saw the last wagon going out of sight on the other side of the clearing. There was nothing for us to do but take their trail, which we did, and followed it for three days. I don't remember anything on this trip except that fellow wouldn't leave me. It seemed to me he would begin to pick at me to get up and come on as soon as I lay down, but I know he would let me lay a reasonable time and then urge me on. But I was so tired and weak that I wanted to be left alone, and I told him to go on and leave me alone. I talked as mean as I knew how, but he stuck to me until we came to the regiment the third day about noon. They were camped beside the road we were following. They had marched across in one night from where we had left them. I was so glad to see them, I lay down and slept the rest of that day.

The next day I dug some hazlebrush root and blackberry roots, steeped them, and made a weak tea that I drank instead of water. There were lots of ripe blackberries near camp, and I would pick an oyster can (that I had put a bail in and used to make coffee in) full of berries, stew and sweeten them, and eat them with my hardtack. I soon got well and as strong as ever, and finally got ashamed and reported to the sergeant for duty. He said, "Yes, I think you are fit, but I had orders not to put you on until you reported." That made me feel more kindly toward the lieutenant than I had before.

I never knew the name of that man that stuck by me, nor even the company he belonged to, and never saw him again to know him. I don't think I would have known him the next day, and never thought of thanking him for staying by me. I would have done the same for him though, and thought nothing of it, as we were comrades and owed it to each other. But I don't believe now that I would ever have gotten around alone.

The first duty was on the skirmish or picket line which was on one side of the Chattahoochee River, with the Rebs on the other side behind a strong line of breastworks about seventy rods from us. We asked the men we relieved if the Rebs were in those works. They said, "Yes."

We asked, "Don't they shoot?"

They said, "No, and we let them alone as long as they do us."

But we were different. So we built a barricade of rails to protect us from their bullets and a shade from the sun. There were four of us. Two did the shooting and the other two loaded the guns. The Rebs had head logs on their works, which were logs about a foot through layed on skids three or four inches through so they could shoot in under the log and the log covered their heads from our sights, also from our bullets. The shade hid our heads so they couldn't see us, but was no protection from their bullets. We could see where our bullets struck when we hit the ground, as the dust would fly, but they couldn't see where they were shooting as it was woods behind us.

We shot until we got the range so we could make the dust fly just on top of the works. But they wouldn't shoot back, so we waited for them to show themselves. About noon we saw the relief coming. We could see their guns glisten above the works, and took a shot at them. Two men got out of the works and started to the rear. One had a red shirt, the other a white shirt. The one with the red shirt was a little ahead and to the left of the other. I told Pat Beaty[5] to take the white shirt, and we fired together. The red shirt went down. The other cut and run, and was out of sight before we could change guns. We soon got a shot from them which went between us and clipped the leaves on our shade. We both shot at the smoke of his gun, which must have been what was called a squirrel rifle, as the bullet slipped through the air as if greased. He must have known the range to perfection too, as every shot came mighty close to center of our rail pile and just over it. One shot came so close to my right cheek as to make a red streak across my cheek. After that we had more respect for him and ducked our heads as soon as we saw the smoke of his gun, but kept shooting at where we saw his smoke until he quit shooting and wouldn't shoot any more. I told Pat if that fellow had known

[5] Patrick Beaty, Hixton, Jackson County, enlisted February 29, 1864; mustered out October 9, 1865. Houghton, p. 42.

how close he was shooting he wouldn't have quit; but we may have got him, as I know we were putting them close and were shooting four balls to his one.

They were evidently state militia as they had different-colored clothes and all kinds of guns. The next post above us could see them drilling near an old cotton gin about a mile back where we thought they were quartered. One of the sergeants went back and got one of those little Rodman guns to come out. They threw three shells at the cotton gin. That broke up their drilling, and they got out of sight in a hurry.

The next duty was farther up the river, where we had to get in before daylight and couldn't get out until dark the next night, and had to keep our heads down or get bullets through them. The Rebs were so close we could hear them talk, but couldn't tell what they said. There was just the river between us. We would put our hat on the ramrod and raise it above the dirt, and a hole was punched through it. So we knew it wouldn't do to raise our heads above the dirt. We would stick our guns over and shoot at random, and a shower of bullets would sprinkle us with dirt.

The trench was about six feet long and so shallow we couldn't stand up. It was on the south slope of the ridge and the sun beat down something fierce. We had to curl up like rats in a hole. The water in our canteens became so warm it wouldn't quench our thirst, but we had to drink it to wash down our hardtack. This was the most disagreeable day I ever put in, in the service or anywhere else, and we were glad when it got dark so we could stand up and stretch out our legs.

Our camp was a half-mile back. One day General Leggett and escort came along. When he stopped and listened, there was no firing in front, so he sent an aide over the hill to see the cause. He found the boys having a talk with the Johnnies, as we called them. They were blackguarding each other. It made the General mad. He said he didn't put them up there to talk but to shoot, and ordered every man be given one hundred rounds, and if they didn't use them up, they were to be put on extra duty. It was impossible to shoot them away, so they threw them away. But it broke up the fun, and the guns were popping all the while in the daytime.

Our rations had been getting shorter ever since we left the Tennessee River, but now they were a joke, one hardtack a day with a small piece of bacon, sugar, and coffee. There were blackberries in places, but we were not allowed to go out of sight of camp, as we didn't know what moment we would be ordered to some other part of the line.

We had a man, Perry Graham,[6] who was a teamster, mule skinner as we called them. The teams were some way back in the rear. Graham got the wagon master's permission to go out and get green corn, and every few

[6] Evidently Oliver P. Graham, Black River Falls, Jackson County, enlisted October 26, 1861; taken prisoner, June 27, 1864; mustered out October 9, 1865. Houghton, p. 40.

days he would fetch up a sack of green corn to us. Oh, how good that corn tasted!

Graham was a tall, well-built man but an oddity. He had a large mouth, square jaws, thin lips, large gray eyes, thin-scattering fuzzy whiskers that looked as if they had been sunburned, and light yellowish hair that he never combed. When excited, he could look fierce and ugly, his eyes would bug out and fairly snap, but when he saw he was beat or it was a joke, his face would change in an instant to the most silly grin. He was fearless and a good pal. One day he went for corn, but didn't come back until some six or eight months later. This is the story he told. He hitched his mule to the rail fence, got over in the corn field, and as the corn was just getting big enough to boil, had to pick some distance away from the mule before he got his sack full. When he tied it up, shouldered it, went to the mule, and threw the sack on the fence, there stood four Rebs with their guns in their hands. They told him to surrender, and began laughing at him, so he told them, "Well, boys, I guess you have got me this time." He said they laughed all the way to camp, said they used him well. He was sent to Andersonville, but soon from there to Libby Prison, where he was kept until the war closed. But, oh, how we missed the big gunnysack of corn.

I have spoken of our camp. Our camp was wherever we stopped. We had no tents, would stack arms, and the ground was our bed and the sky our cover. We often slept with our belts on and gun by our side, ready to fall in at a moment's warning. Two men were detailed to go back in the rear, where they could get wood and water, to make coffee and boil the beef when we got beef, and bring it up to us at the front. But when on a march, each man had his coffee and a little pail made of an oyster can with a wire bail of our own make, to make coffee in, and half a canteen for a frying pan. At the front we couldn't have a fire, nor get water.

When we left here, we went southeast, around the Rebs' right flank, our regiment in advance with Company F ahead as skirmishers. They were mostly Indians. About noon they ran onto some Rebs and had a lively little scrap with them. We were drawn up in line of battle off to one side of the road, just behind a low ridge. The brigadier, with his staff, was on the ridge watching the scrap with his field glasses, his orderly holding his horse. A stray bullet hit the orderly in the right shoulder. He hollered, "Oh!" and ran squarely in front of our regiment, hollered "Oh!" every step until he fell forward on his face, the "oh" fainter and fainter every step. Several men ran from the left of our regiment to meet him, but he fell before they got to him. He was dead when they did get to him. He was a nice-appearing young man and well known by all the boys as the General's orderly. The skirmish was soon over, and we resumed our march to the southeast.

I think the above was on the nineteenth of July, 1864, and on the twenty-first, about noon, we heard heavy firing in advance. We hurried forward. When going down a gentle slope about half a mile from the front, we saw an ambulance coming on a run. It passed two Sisters of Charity a few rods ahead, and there was a man in it with both legs shot off above the knees. It was a bloody sight. A man was on each side hanging to the ambulance to keep up. I heard one ask him if he had any word to send home. I presume they were newspaper reporters as they had citizen's clothes on. I thought what a sight for those Sisters, and so close to the front.

We were on reserve that day, but after dark, we relieved the regiment in front. They had charged the Rebs' rifle pits just before dark, and were repulsed. They had then dug in and had quite a bank of dirt. We finished it and lay down to sleep. When it was getting light next morning, we were awakened by our officers, cautioned not to make any noise, climbed over the breastworks and started across the corn field for the Rebs. We saw several dead men that had been killed the night before. But when we got to the rifle pits, they were empty. The Rebs were gone, and we knew our officers were fooled. But I was glad there were no Rebs in those pits.

We were on a ridge with some timber on it. I could see Atlanta some four miles to the west. We sat and stood around until about ten o'clock when the lieutenant told me to go and hurry the cooks up with the coffee. I gave him my gun and belts and went for the cooks. When about halfway, I heard some shooting back in that direction. I soon met the major's hostler. He said the Rebs were coming up in our rear. I told him we were going to have our beef for supper. But when I got to where the cooks had been, I saw them going into the woods to the north.

This was in a ravine running nearly north and south with quite a high ridge on each side. I saw troops coming from the north on the ridge to the east, also artillery on the run. The infantry formed lines of battle up and down the hill a little above me facing an open field to the south. The artillery unit worked on the ridge, and covered the guns with brush. There was a fort on the ridge west that had been made the day before. They were pulling the guns out and pointing them to the rear. I went up there. They said there would soon be fun there, so I stopped to see the fun. Soon our skirmishers fell back across the field. When the Rebs pushed to the edge of the woods, they stopped until their line came up, then all advanced. When halfway across, our men opened fire. I saw the Reb flag go down three times. It was picked up, but they fell back. The dust and smoke soon hid them, and I thought there would be fun on the other side next, so started back for my regiment as fast as I could go.

About one hundred yards from where my regiment was, there was a ravine running nearly southwest. I saw General McPherson and an orderly going up that ravine to the southwest. I ran every step to where the regiment was. When I got there, they told me Mc-Pherson was killed. I wouldn't believe it, but it was too true.

As I got there, the Rebs opened with artillery and we got into the rifle pits the Rebs had left. I asked the lieutenant where my gun and belts were. He had set them beside a tree some ten rods from where we were.

I said, "I'm not going out there after them."

He said, "No, there will be extra guns soon."

But soon the Rebs stopped throwing shell. They gave me some shovels and picks to take back to the rear, so I left with them. I hadn't gone far when they opened again, and the cannon balls were flying all around me. They would hit the ground and bound up like rubber balls. I ran the best I knew. Sandy Green of my company went by me on a short-tail mare, and he was putting the spurs to her. That short tail was rolling round and round, and Green was looking over first one shoulder then the other. His eyes fairly stuck out. He was the most scared-looking fellow I ever saw. I don't think he saw me. I had to laugh and came to a walk.

When I got to the trench, I left the shovels and picks with a guard and went on up the hill to the main road. I thought to hunt the cooks. I went half a mile when I met General Logan with two regiments, one armed with sixteen-shot guns, the other with seven-shot carbines. I heard Logan say he would have McPherson's body if he sacrificed every man in the Fifteenth Corps, so I followed them back. They went up the same ravine

I had seen General McPherson go. I stopped with the guard where I had left the shovels, and those regiments made an awful popping up in the woods for about a minute. Then all was quiet, so I started for my regiment. When halfway I met the ambulance with a file of soldiers on each side with McPherson's body.

When I got back to the regiment, all was quiet, but they had had quite a lively time while I had been gone. Just after I left, the Rebs charged them, first in the front, then in the rear. They said had they come from both sides at the same time, they would have gobbled them. But they stood them off. The artillery company had howitzers up behind my company as the Rebs were coming from the front. Our boys were lying down and about thirty feet in front of the artillery when they fired. It was loaded with grape and canister. One man had his knapsack in front of his head. It took his hat and knapsack off and he never found either, although he went out quite a way. So the boys wouldn't have them shoot over them again, but ran it in front of them.

When I got back, I went out in front and found my gun and belts beside the tree where the lieutenant had left them. My son Emerson has that gun now. But the fight was over for that day. I think this was called the Battle of Peach Tree Creek. It quieted down to picket or skirmish firing the next few days.

The next day I went up in the woods where McPherson was killed. I saw one place where the dead Rebs were piled three deep, and they were scattered quite thick as far as we could see through the woods, which was quite thick.

The next few days there was only skirmish firing. About noon the twenty-sixth of July we were ordered to be ready to march at a moment's notice. We packed our things and got on our belts, but it was near night before we got started. We had eaten the last hardtack that morning, but the teams were back on the rear so we went without for the next two days. We marched that night, and the next day about noon made a halt. The cooks were along and had coffee enough to make one mess, but it wasn't ground so they put it in whole. When it was nearly boiling, we were ordered to fall in, so each took his tin cup full and drank it on the way. It couldn't be called coffee as it was barely colored, but I was about the last so I got my cup half-full of the coffee, and I ate the coffee after I had drunk the water.

Near night we ran onto the Rebs. The pickets drove them back about half a mile and went to digging in. We worked at building breastworks nearly all night, but as soon as it began to get light, we climbed over and advanced about a mile. We took up a position on quite a high ridge in an open field in the rear. We were on reserve. We stacked arms and carried rails up to the line in front, and they too were digging mighty lively, for they could see the Rebs preparing to charge. They charged three times that day, but our boys had a fair line of breastworks by the time they charged the last time, and the dead Rebs were thick in front.

93

We had to go a half-mile to the right, where there was a vacancy in the line, and we double-quicked over there. But we had been there only a few minutes when the regiment that belonged there came, and we went back to our place. We had just gotten back when we saw our cook coming up across the open field with a box of hardtack on his shoulder, and he looked good to us. This was the third day since we had eaten anything,[7] and we gave him a lusty cheer and made a hole in that box in short order. How the other companies cursed their cooks for not coming too. But they came about dark when the firing had quieted down.

Shortly after the cook got there, a shower of cannon balls came over the hill to the right of us, not over four to six rods in our rear, nearly parallel with our line. Some were rolling on the ground. Some of our boys started to catch them but were ordered back, and were told if they put out their foot, the ball would take the foot off. But it was a sight to see them. They came bounding along so thick one couldn't count a quarter of them. They were solid shot. They had been thrown at one of our batteries over the hill, so were pretty well spent as they passed us.

[7] In his *Personal Memoirs*, II, 534–35, U. S. Grant says of Sherman's army as it marched in review in Washington, D. C., May 24, 1865: "Sherman's army was not so well dressed as the Army of the Potomac, but their marching could not be excelled; they gave the appearance of men who had been thoroughly drilled to endure hardships, either by long and continuous marches or through exposure to any climate, without the ordinary shelter of a camp." The above indicates why they would make such an impression.

We had learned from prisoners taken the twenty-second that General J. B. Hood had superseded General Joseph E. Johnston in command of the Rebs and had said that the Army of the Tennessee had never been whipped, and he was going to give them one good whipping if he sacrificed every man in his command. We were a part of the Army of the Tennessee. Some five months later he did sacrifice his command at Franklin and Nashville.

They were badly repulsed the twenty-eighth, and fell back to the works around Atlanta. We moved a little farther to the right and nearer town, and built a good breastworks. This was northwest of the city. We just got them done when we were marched out and saw another regiment take our place. It made us sore to build works for others to fight behind.

We went farther to the right and built another line facing an open field with head logs on top to protect our heads, but the Rebs didn't charge us any more. A few days later we advanced across that field and built another line. We carried those head logs across the field to the new line by moonlight. The sharpshooters made it disagreeable in the daytime.

A big gun near town disturbed our sleep at night. There was a ridge and timber between us and town, and they had the advantage of our skirmishers and us in the breastworks as well. A number of the boys had close calls. One day as the cook was dealing out coffee and meat, I was sitting on the bank on the back side of the trench. A boy, Turner was his name, was against my knees with his plate in one hand and cup in the other, waiting for his turn. A bullet came over the works and hit him in the left shoulder blade, but didn't come through. If it had, I wouldn't be writing this. He fell back with cup and plate still in his hands, but gave them up when told. He looked first at one, then at another as they picked him up and carried him down the trench where it was in the timber out of sight of the Rebs and put him on a stretcher. They opened his shirt to give him air. He said, "Boys what's the matter? What makes it so hard for me to breathe?" And they didn't get ten rods when he was dead.

This made us more careful. We suspected some Johnnie had climbed a tree, and one of the boys saw the smoke of his gun. They went back where the battery was, and the artilleryman located him with his field glasses. The second shell knocked him out of the tree. It was about a mile from the gun, and no more Rebs climbed trees, which was a great relief to us.

We built our bunks just back of the trench with shades over to keep the sun off in the day and dew off at night. But that big gun over toward Atlanta would throw a shell over once in a while. The most of them went clear over us, but one very dark night when we were asleep, one came and knocked the shed down about twenty feet from where I was asleep. When I awoke, all were talking, and I asked the man I was sleeping with what they were all talking for.

He said, "Didn't you hear that shell burst?"

I said, "No."

He said, "You must have been dead!"

But it didn't hurt a man and I was soon asleep again. We got so we had little respect for those shells, but they made a big noise as they were 125-pounders and we could hear them coming before they got to us. It seemed as if they were coming right where we were.

When we left here, we went on a big march to the southwest and struck the railroad running west from Atlanta. The troops ahead had torn up the rails, piled the ties up, set them afire, heated the rails red hot, and wound them around trees. It was said this was done for about fifteen miles.

An incident that I should have spoken of happened the next day after the twenty-second of July. We heard cheering off to our right, and wondered what it was about. As there was no unusual firing, we knew it wasn't a charge. But soon we saw General W. T. Sherman and some of his aides coming up the line, and when opposite our command the boys began to cheer him. He took off his hat and faced us, and all was quiet in an instant. In a few words he thanked us for the way we had conducted ourselves the day before, and lamented the death of McPherson. Then he rode on to the next command, and we heard the cheering as he greeted other commands to the left until it died away in the distance. We thought more of him for those few words, and I want to say that he was liked by all of his

men. He was a nice-appearing man, though not handsome. He was one of us, no pomp nor stuck-up, but
common, every-day, and right on the job all the while.

I will resume the story of our march to the right. The
country which we passed through was heavily tim-
bered and thinly settled. It had not been run over by
either army. We camped one night early as we were
in the advance. I saw a house some distance back from
the road, and some apple trees near it. They were loaded
with nice-looking apples, and Ed Markey[8] and I went
over there to get some, but Mos Brick, an Indian, and
two boys of the Seventeenth Wisconsin were there
beside the house talking. We went on by them as the
apples were on the side of the house. Near the north
end of the house were about twelve stands of bees. We
went through a bridle gate to get to the apples, which
were west of the bees, and there was a rail fence between the bees and apples.

The ground under the trees was covered with apples,
and I went to picking them up in my hat, as also did Ed.
I had my hat nearly full when a bee lit on my cheek,
and I knew he was mad the way he performed. I knew
if I held the muscle of my face still until I got away
from the hives he wouldn't sting. So I began to turn
to get away, but he stung and I brushed him off and
made for the woods some rods away to the north. I had

[8] Edward H. Markey, Black River Falls, Jackson County, enlisted November 5, 1861; musician; mustered out October 9, 1865.
Houghton, p. 40.

to pass near Ed and he thought I was crazy, as he said my head was as big as a bushel basket. So he grabbed me and went too, whipping the bees off me with his hat until the bees stung him in the ears so that he had to let me go and he made for the woods. There was an old road running up the hill. I dove into the first thick brush and lay still with my face down. Ed didn't see where I went, he was so busy, but knew I went up the road, so he ran past me. When he got to the top of the hill and couldn't see me, he hollered. I told him to get in the brush and lay down, but he came back where I was still fighting the bees. I told him to lay still, and the bees soon left us, but we didn't have any apples.

We went back to the edge of the woods when we saw Prosser. He was a fifer. Ed Markey was a drummer, so was well acquainted with him. I hollered to Prosser, but Ed said, "Keep still and we will see some fun." Prosser went to the same trees I had been at, but didn't pick many apples when you would have thought a cyclone had struck him. He went twice around the tree, both hands flying, then started for the house. But when he came to the fence, he saw where the bees came from. He took back across the field the way he had come, and I never say anyone run as he did. His hands were flying over his head like the wings of a bird. It didn't look like he touched the ground, and he was out of sight in the woods in no time.

We concluded we didn't want apples. Ed was stung worse than I was, but I had all I wanted, only one sting

in my face, but the back of my neck and head was pep-
pered so full it was numb. We took a wide circuit
around to the east of the house and found some sweet
potatoes. We got our hats full and went to camp. We
didn't see anyone at the house. I presume there were
only women at home and they were scared to come out.

We learned later what had made the bees so mad.
That Indian had told those Seventeenth Wisconsin
boys how to get the honey. The hives were about two
feet high and some sixteen inches square, with notches
at the bottom for the bees to go in and out. Also there
were two round holes halfway up the hive. He told
them to put their thumb over one of the holes and punch
the bees to death with a stick through the other hole.
Then he peeked around the corner of the house, and
those boys punched the bees until nearly blind with the
bees, and tipped two houses over getting away.

After crossing the railroad, we went south, I think
some thirty miles, and struck the railroad running south
to Macon, Georgia. The Rebs were there to meet us.
There were other troops ahead and we were marched
out to one side of the road, and other troops that were
behind went by us among whom was a regiment of
Zouaves of New York. They had new uniforms and
looked as if they had just come out of a bandbox. It was
a large regiment and they were nearly on the double-
quick. There was a lively scrap ahead, but we didn't
get into it. It was something new for us to see other
troops go ahead and we sit beside the road, but it was

said they feared an attack from Atlanta, so we were to guard the rear. The musket firing was heavy, but not much artillery, and it soon died down to picket firing. This was the last railroad into Atlanta, and that night we saw a big fire shine up on the sky, and big explosions in that direction. The Twentieth Corps had been left in front of Atlanta. They were strongly fortified, and they took possession the next day. This fight was near Jonesboro, Georgia.

We camped about a mile back from the Rebels' works in a piece of timber. The ground in front was a little higher, so we couldn't see the works, but could hear the firing. There was a nice creek a few rods behind camp in a deep gulch, with a fine white sand bottom, and water about two inches deep. One day I went down there to scour my gun barrel. I went by where one of the Company D boys was shaving one of the other boys. I was gone about an hour, and when I got back the one that was doing the shaving was buried. A ball had come from the front and killed him instantly. He never spoke, but fell backwards on his back and held the razor in his hand until told to let go. I couldn't believe or realize it when they told me. That was the only bullet that came in this camp, and he, like Turner, didn't know he was hit.

A good many of the boys were getting what the doctor called "jiggers," the forerunner of scurvy, from not having vegetables, and we were given one onion to the company. It was a large flat one, nearly as big around as a tea saucer, and looked awfully nice. The boys said they could eat it alone, but there was enough for the whole company as it had been pickled in red pepper and vinegar and was the hottest onion I ever tasted. But we ate the whole of it, the boys trying to see who could eat the biggest piece, and there wasn't a dry eye in camp.

Then they issued fresh beef. It was so poor that there wouldn't be a bead of grease on a whole kettle after it was boiled, and they gave us what was called "desecrated vegetables." This looked and tasted as if it had been scum off a farmer's swill barrel. The boys wouldn't have eaten it in the first year of the war, but all ate it now and called it good. Anything that might stop hunger was good.

When we left here, we went back to within three miles of Atlanta. We got our mail here which we hadn't had for about a month. I had about seven dollars in money I had carried about three months, but couldn't buy a chew of tobacco, nor anything to eat. We hadn't been here an hour when one of the Twentieth Corps teamsters came on a mule with about half a box of plug tobacco on the saddle pommel. We knew this was Rebel tobacco, but he asked ten cents a chew. I heard one of the boys tell Major Worden, and Worden said, "If you want tobacco, I should think you ought to know how to get it." So I followed down to see what was going to happen.

One went up to the man on the mule and told him if he couldn't sell his tobacco more reasonably, he had better get out of camp. The fellow said in a defiant tone, "I will sell my tobacco as I please." The boys grabbed him and the tobacco and pulled them off the mule, the mule going out of the way. The whole crowd piled on top, all clawing for the tobacco. The box had been knocked off the tobacco, and it looked like a big pile of maggots as they all clawed for the center where the tobacco was. There was a wash-out a few feet below, some three or four feet deep, and into it the whole mass rolled and tumbled, clawing and tumbling, not a word from anyone. Those that were kicked out at bottom jumped in the top and were clawed down through the pile again. I saw how it was working, so took off my hat and jumped on the pile. I had to shut my eyes and mouth to keep the dust and dirt out, and kept my face as close down to my breast as I could, as I had done when the bees were after me. My right hand soon got hold of a plug of tobacco and I gave it a yank. I stuffed it in my shirt bosom, and just as I was being kicked out at the bottom I got another plug. So I got up on the bank, put on my hat, brushed the dirt off my face and clothes the best I could, and said, "I didn't want tobacco anyway. I just wanted to see how it would feel to go through that mass."

The man that had been so defiant with his tobacco was standing up on the bank looking at the squirming mass below. His pockets were wrong side out, his hat gone, the buttons nearly all off his clothes, and just as dirty as the rest who had been through the mill, and was perfectly tame. One of the boys had caught his mule and was holding it a little way off. When the mass in the ditch had dissolved, he found his hat, got on his mule without thanking the man for holding it, and rode off, wiser if not richer than when he came. After this we were called Worden's Mob.

I went up to camp and the boys had put up our tent, which we hadn't seen for several months, and the mail had come also, and I got two pounds of tobacco which my sister had sent me from La Crosse, Wisconsin. So I cut the Reb tobacco up and gave it to the boys. It was rank, very strong tobacco, but they were glad to get anything that looked like tobacco. I didn't have a knapsack, so told Bill Dailey[9] if he would carry that which my sister had sent, he could use it as long as it lasted.

On the march from Jonesboro, a man of my company, who had been poorly for a long time, was excused by the doctor from duty so he could start out with the advance and have all day to get to camp. He could sit down and rest when he liked. About noon we passed him. He was sitting in the shade beside the road, looking as well as usual, but that was the last we ever heard of him. He was the man who had his cartridge belt knocked off him by a shell at Shiloh which also tore the shoulder of his coat out. Think I spoke of it before.[10]

[9] William Dailey, La Crosse, enlisted February 26, 1864; mustered out October 9, 1865. Houghton, p. 42.

[10] Edgar P. Houghton (p. 43) in his roster of company names shows one Carl Richembach of Albion, Jackson County, who en-

We drew a ration of flour here, and as we had no way to make bread, the lieutenant said if three men and a corporal would volunteer to take it down to Atlanta and trade it for bread, he would give us a pass. So three men, and I as corporal, went. It was near night, but as there was a good moon, we could come back by moonlight. Just as we got to the edge of town we met a patrol —a corporal and three men. He looked at our pass, and said, "This is too old." It was dated the day before. I told him what we were there for, and we had the sack of flour, but he said he would have to take us to headquarters, though he thought the lieutenant would pass us. It was on our way to the bakery.

When I told the lieutenant my story, he told us to go inside. He was sitting on a bench on the sidewalk just outside the door. We went in and sat on a bench near the window. Soon another patrol came with a man that had no pass. He was dressed up and took off his hat and scraped his foot on the walk, begged the lieutenant's pardon, and said if he would let him go this time, he wouldn't be caught out without a pass again, and he let him go. I saw where I had made a mistake and it made me sore. I went to the door and demanded I be taken to the provost marshal at once. He said, "In a few minutes," and when taken to the provost office, there was only a clerk who took our names and put us

listed December 18, 1863, as "Left sick on march from Jonesboro, Georgia, September 7, '64." This would seem to be the man referred to.

upstairs in the courthouse. They kept us here twenty-four hours. This was the first time I was ever put in the guardhouse. They worked half of us on the street in the forenoon, and the other half in the afternoon.

There were some twenty-five or thirty in the guardhouse, all strangers to us, but all soldiers. They took us out just at dusk of evening and lined us up on the lawn. An officer told us we could go. I asked him if he wasn't going to give us a pass to get out of town.

He said, "No."

I said, "How do we know we won't be arrested again before we get a block from here?"

He said, "That is your lookout."

I said, "We'll look out."

He said, "Don't get sassy."

I made no reply, as I knew it wouldn't do to talk back to a shoulder strap, and told the boys to come on. We had had a fine view of the city from the upper story of the courthouse, as it was on the highest ground in town. We made for the depot, where I had heard there was a soldiers' home for soldiers who had been in the hospital and were returning to their regiments. When out on the sidewalk, which was made of brick, we found a place where a shell had broken it up. We took a half-brick in each hand and started for the depot, and if we had met a patrol we couldn't reason with, they would have found out how heavy those bricks were. But we didn't meet any. We went to the soldiers' home and told them we had just come in and wanted to know where our regiment was. They told us we could stay until morning, so we registered, got our supper, breakfast, and lodging free. I got paper, pen, and ink to write a letter home, took them to our room, and copied the pass we had, giving it the right date. But we didn't meet a patrol to show it to.

The trains were putting out for Chattanooga, and I told the boys if they would go with me, we would climb on and try to get to the regiment, which was at De Valls Bluff, Arkansas, the last we had heard. King and Fuller[11] of my company said they would go, but George Miller, a Company H man, was afraid we would be arrested as deserters and wouldn't go. I knew it wouldn't do for us three to go and let him go back to the detachment and tell where we had gone, so we traded the flour for bread and started for camp. Just out of town we met some of the boys the lieutenant had sent to find us.

We lay in this camp I think about two weeks. It might have been longer. That was nearly sixty-three years ago, and I am writing this from pure memory, and with no way to get dates. I only remember what impressed me most, but what I write is the truth, while I don't pretend to tell all the truth. This is the fifteenth

[11] There were three men by the name of King in Company I: Charles H., from Hixton, Jackson County, and George R. and John F., from Neillsville, Clark County. This was probably Charles H. King, who enlisted about the same time as Relyea. The other two enlisted somewhat later. The Fuller referred to was probably Moses K. Fuller of Hixton, Jackson County, who enlisted February 19, 1864, and was mustered out October 9, 1865. Houghton, p. 43.

of July, 1927, and I was eighty-one the twenty-eighth of June.

A. L. Reylea came to us here out of the hospital at Rome, Georgia, where he had been left on our way down here. He had the typhoid fever and had recovered fully. He, Bill Dailey, Ben Folsom,[12] and I tented together the rest of our service.

When we left here, we went north. The Rebs had gone around us to the west and struck one line near Kennesaw Mountain, and we were sent to drive them off. They tore up about fifteen miles of track by tipping it over. It stopped the trains only a short time as all our men had to do was tip it back.

On our way we stopped one day about noon near Marietta, where the Tenth Wisconsin was provost. Gerald and Ed Markey and I went over to their camp as all of that regiment was from Black River Falls and Ed was acquainted with the most of them. We ate dinner with them. They had a table rigged up with benches to sit on, which was quite a treat to us. We hadn't eaten at a table in a long time, and it was a long time before we did again.

When we got back to Allatoona Pass, the Rebs had left there the day before. This is where Sherman signaled to General Corse from the top of Kennesaw Mountain to "Hold the fort, I am coming!" He did hold the fort, to the Rebs' sorrow. He only had a small bri-

---

[12] Benjamin Folsom, Springfield, Jackson County, enlisted January 13, 1864; mustered out October 9, 1865. Houghton, p. 43.

gade of three or four regiments. There was a big shed full of hardtack here, but the Rebs didn't get it as it was too close to the fort. We didn't get any either, but marched by it. But on this march we got all the corn we wanted. Nearly every day when we went into camp, it was a sight to look ahead. Every man would have six or eight ears of corn tied to his bayonet, with here or there a pumpkin stuck on a bayonet. If a man got a pumpkin, he was lucky and had a treat. The corn was dent corn and hard enough to grate. We made graters out of half of a canteen, and a frying pan of the other half. We spread our rubber blanket on the ground and put the grater on it and soon grated corn enough for supper and breakfast. We made mush of it for supper and fried it for breakfast. We got a fair ration of sugar and coffee, and a small piece of bacon, or sow bosom as some called it, but no hardtack if we could get corn.

We followed the Rebs nearly to the Tennessee River, where we stopped several days. Here we drew three days' rations, and Reylea sat down and ate the whole three days' ration except the coffee, which was given the cook to make for the company; but he ate his sugar and crackers. I asked him what he would do tomorrow. He said, "Let tomorrow take care of itself. I am going to eat, drink, and be merry, for tomorrow I may die." But the next day he was detailed to go out after forage for the mules, and he got his haversack full of wheat, the only wheat I had seen in the South. We boiled it. We had some sugar that belonged to the mess—the four of us messed together—and we sweetened the wheat, and it made good eating. The next day we went out a little way from camp and found lots of wild crabapples. They were green and as hard as stones. We boiled a kettle of them until they were soft, but our sugar was gone and those crabs were sour and puckery, and about the poorest excuse for grub I ever ate. The boys said they would pucker our stomachs to fit our rations. We ate all we wanted of them, and they didn't hurt us.

I used to like to take a walk out in the woods all alone where I could get out of the noise of camp, hear the birds sing, and see now and then a gray squirrel run up a tree and bark at me, and on this march several times found nuts to satisfy my hunger. One time I found where there had been a few hills of peanuts planted. I didn't know what they were until I pulled a hill up. I think there was a quart of peanuts on that one hill. I sat down and broke one open. It tasted like a raw bean, but I kept chewing, and the longer I chewed the better it tasted. I filled up on those raw peanuts, and I have liked raw peanuts ever since.

Another time we found a big chestnut tree that had just begun to drop the nuts. We cut the tree down and there were a lot of nuts on it. We had to pick them out of the burs with our pocket knives, but they were the best chestnuts I ever ate. There were ten or twelve nuts in some burs. The burs were as big around as a baseball. They had sharp spines or prickers on them, so one had to work carefully or get his fingers pricked.

At another time I came to a small creek and on a riffle saw a school of minnows. They were two to three inches long, and were as thick as they could be. Near by was an old rail fence. The water was shallow, so I laid a rail above and another below them, went to camp and got a pail. I told Adam I was going fishing. He came along, and he got on one rail and I on the other, and we scooped them up with our two hands until we had all we wanted. We went to camp, I borrowed a frying pan, fried the grease out of a piece of bacon, got it good and hot and went in the tent. There sat Adam with a small pair of scissors cleaning fish. He was snipping off the little fins, tail and head, and taking out the inwards. I set the frying pan on the ground and scooped up two hands full of the live minneys and put them in the hot grease. Adam looked at me as though he thought I had gone crazy.

He said, "What in thunder are you doing?"

I said, "Frying fish."

He said, "Well, by gosh, you can eat them!"

I told him he could dress what he wanted to eat and I would fry his separately, but he had lost all interest in the fish, put his scissors away, and would have no more to do with them. I was sorry he had taken it so to heart, but he had been in the hospital all summer and wasn't as famished as we were. If he hadn't seen them put in the hot grease, he wouldn't have known but what they were dressed, for they were fine. But he wouldn't look at us while we were eating them, and years afterward when I told of it he said, "Lish done that so he could get all the fish."

CHAPTER V

SEEKING THE REGIMENT
IN THE WEST

One day I told the boys that I wouldn't go back to Atlanta.

"Neither will I," Adam[1] said.

But I said, "I am not boasting. I mean what I say."

"So do I," Adam said.

I said we would go a half-mile, and "if they go toward Atlanta, we'll leave them the first brush we come to."

Adam said, "All right."

This had been in my mind ever since they had worked us on the street in Atlanta, which had made me very sore. They had used us first on one flank, then the other. They wouldn't give us clothing because we hadn't officers to receive it from them, as nearly all our officers had left us, and they had put officers out of other regiments over us. Lieutenant Manley had gone to the hospital, so we supposed, but learned different later. So when we left here we started back the way we had come.

We were behind the train, but the other regiment was behind us. We stopped after just about a half-mile.

[1] Adam Relyea.

Then Reylea and I left and took to the brush. We didn't get far when I thought of my tobacco in Bill's[2] knapsack, and Adam had seven dollars in Ben Folsom's pocketbook. So we went back to get that. When Bill saw that I took half of the tobacco, he wanted to know what I meant, and I had to tell him, and told him to keep still. But he went with me, and when we got to where Adam was to meet me, Ben was with him. There were four of us, and Ben had the company coffee and kettles. We dasn't take that back, so took it along and traded it at the first house we came to.

These three men were what we called recruits, as they had enlisted in the fall or winter of '63 or '64 and came to us in April, 1864, at Vicksburg, Mississippi. They had been with us at the front since, but they looked to me to take the lead.

I had intended to strike the Tennessee River, steal a boat, and go down that river to Cairo, Illinois, but the rear of our command had quite a skirmish with the Rebs soon after we left the detachment. We changed our minds and struck for Rome, Georgia. Bill wanted to throw our guns and belts away, but I said no, that I was going to stick to my gun, as I didn't think they could call me a deserter as long as I had my gun and cartridge box, and only wanted to get to the regiment.

About sundown, as we were passing a cross road, a man ran across the road about half a mile to the north of us; then another and another until five or six had

[2] Bill Dailey.

crossed out of the woods into an open field on a ridge. They were scrouched down as if they didn't want to be seen. A cavalryman had overtaken us a little way back and had ridden along with us until we were out of sight of the skulkers. Also eight or ten Negroes that were running away were with us. As soon as the cavalryman had left us, I told the Negroes to hike on ahead. They didn't want to leave us, but I told them, "Go!" So they took a run ahead. Bill wanted to take a shot at those men, as we saw their heads peeking over the hill in the open field. But I said, "No, we will let them alone if they will us." They could see there was quite a squad of us, evidently thinking the cavalryman our officer, and didn't know the most of us were runaway Negroes. Otherwise they might have made it lively for us.

We made for the first thick brush we came to, and made our beds in the middle of it. It was about ten rods from the road. We ate some of the bread we had gotten for the coffee, drank some water out of our canteens, and went to sleep. As soon as it was light the next morning we ate some more of the bread and started out. The road was tracked up by barefooted horses, showing there had been quite a squad of bushwhackers along since we had left the road the evening before. If they had been cavalry, their horses would have been shod. We kept a sharp lookout until we came to the Fourteenth Corps pickets. We learned from them that the Fourteenth Corps had gone on this road the day before. They asked us where we had stayed that night. We told them about three miles back. They said they had had quite a skirmish that morning just at the peep of daylight, but we hadn't heard anything all night. I was satisfied they were the fellows we had seen the night before peeking over the hill at us, and were what they called the Rebs' home guard.

We called it quits then on striking out alone. We knew of a Wisconsin regiment that belonged to the Fourteenth Corps, I have forgotten the number, but we belonged to that regiment until we got by the Fourteenth Corps. We learned that our command was just south of the town, so we then belonged to the Sixteenth Corps and got by the guard on the bridge over into Rome. We heard there that our detachment was about a mile south of town, and Ben Folsom thought we had better go back to them; but I said I would not go back unless taken back under guard, but was going to my regiment if possible. And I asked Ben, "What would you do going back without the kettles and coffee you traded for bread? They would mob you." So that settled it.

We found they were moving the hospital back to Chattanooga, and were loading box cars. This was the end of a branch running out from Kingston, which was on the main line. We hung around until it was getting dark, then climbed into an empty box car, and made our beds with our guns and belts for pillows. When we heard someone come, and he stuck his lantern in the door, we were groaning. He passed on and we were soon on the way to Kingston, where the engineer ran into a box car and smashed his headlight, so we lay there until daylight the next morning. Here there was a train from Atlanta with a lot of soldiers on top of the box cars. I went over, found out their story, and went back and told the boys to come on as we belonged to that squad. We climbed on and were soon on our way to Chattanooga.

This was the worst ride I ever took on anything, but we enjoyed it as we were on our way to the regiment. It was rough, mountainous country, and the road was as rough as the country. It was crooked and there were lots of bridges. We saw three whole trains that had left the track that summer. They had run clear off the track, the engines burned halfway up the boiler, the cars right side up and looked as if they were coupled together, but had been unloaded. We crept up hill all day. At times we would strike a down grade where they would go flying fast enough. That box car would roll and bound along at a fearful rate. Then we would have to hang to the foot board to keep from being shaken off, and shut our eyes to keep the cinders and smoke out of them.

As it began to get dark at night we came to where there was a side track. They left half of the train here. We were on the front half, and they crept up the hill with it, the engine puffing and snorting at a fearful rate. They had to stop several times, to let it rest, the boys said, but it was to get up steam: They fired with wood, and it was hard to keep up steam where it was a steady pull with no let up. When we got up to the top, there was a tunnel and another side track. They left us here and went back after the other half of the train. Adam and I went up to the tunnel. It was cut out of the solid rock. Over the mouth of the tunnel was a sign saying the length of the tunnel was 2,229 feet. We went into it until we couldn't see each other, but we couldn't see the other end, and where we had come in was getting to look fearfully small, and the water was dripping down from above. So we went back.

When they came with the other half of the train, they coupled onto us. This put us well back from the engine. It was quite dark now, and they ran slowly until nearly through the tunnel. We had been told to lie down tight or we might get our heads bumped, and we lay down and hung to the foot board all night. I slept some after we got down the hill, but going down that hill was frightful. They ran at a fearful speed, and the road was so crooked it would look as if the engine had surely left the track. It would shoot off at one side out of sight, and when we came to that sharp curve it would give us a jerk. The cinders and smoke were frightful. We were glad when daylight came.

We soon got to Chattanooga, where we found out we had to have transportation. Our bread was gone, and we were hungry after our ride. We went down to an old abandoned brick kiln and talked the situation over. I told them one of us would have to be a sergeant, and he would have to go to the commander of the place, and tell him, "I and three men have been on detached service with Sherman. We were ordered to report to my regiment, and rode on top of the cars last night. I had our orders and transportation in my pocketbook and it worked out of my pocket and shook off the car and my orders and transportation are gone, and I don't know what to do."

I said, "Now Bill Dailey has got a sergeant's cap, but I don't think he will make a good-looking sergeant."

Bill said, "You can take my hat, but I won't go before the commander."

I said, "Nor I either, but Adam will make a fine sergeant. I can make up a reasonable lie, but am not good at telling it, and if I went up he would be sure to catch me."

Adam said, "That is quite a compliment to me, but I will try it."

He was about four years older than I was, and as fine a looking man as there was in the whole army. He was just as straight as a cob, well built, long, wavy hair, and a nice mustache. He was a good talker and perfectly fearless. He took Bill's hat and went while we sat there in the brickyard and waited for him to come back. I knew just as soon as I saw him coming that he had succeeded, for there was a smile on his face and he was stepping high and lively. He said he would tell all the lies I wanted him to. He said the commander sat looking at him after he had told his story, and finally said,

"I don't like to detain men trying to get to their regiment, and will send you along as you are an honest-looking man. I can't give you transportation past another commander, but will give you a recommendation to the commander at Nashville."

He gave him an order for transportation to Nashville and an order to draw rations for himself and three men. We went to the commissary and drew three days' rations, then went back to the brickyard, built a fire, heated some water, and took a good wash. We had gotten a bar of soap, and we hadn't washed our faces and hands since we had started on this trip. We made coffee and ate our fill, then went to the depot and got our transportation to Nashville. We were happy and got on the first train out.

The trains were all box cars, and mostly empties. We soon found the train we were on was a dinkey issuing rations to the guards along the road and stopped every few miles. Several trains passed us. We got to a small town where they issued rations, and Adams came and said he wished we hadn't drawn rations at Chattanooga as they were giving bigger and better rations here. So I said, "What's the matter, why not draw three days' rations here?" He looked at the order the commander had given him and said, "I don't see why we can't," and went and drew three days' rations.

We decided to leave this train and wait for the next one as this one was too slow and might not go clear through to Nashville anyway. Adam found a citizen who wanted to buy some coffee, and we sold him the whole of the ration we had gotten, and we had money enough to buy all the pie and cake we wanted on the rest of this trip.

We soon got another train and got to Nashville early that evening. Adam went up to the commander with his story, or rather my story, and the recommendation the commander at Chattanooga had given him. He said the commander deliberated some time, then shook his head and said, "I don't dare do that, but you report at the barracks tomorrow morning at nine o'clock and you will be sent on." But he didn't say how. He said, "You can go up there tonight if you want to, but I would advise you not to until morning, as it is a pretty rough place, and there is a nice place at the depot." We went up to the barracks, as he called it. It was a large brick building that covered a whole block. It was built for a hotel, but never had been finished. It was called the Zollicoffer House, having been built by General Zollicoffer, who was killed in the fore part of the war, and was being used for a guardhouse.

We found it was a rough, dirty place and no fooling about it. We were in it only a short time when we were taken out under a guard with a lot of others and taken down to the Louisville depot.[3] But the train was full before they got to us as we were in the rear of the squad, so we were taken back to the guardhouse again and kept

[3] Surely he means the Louisville and Nashville Railroad depot; they did not go to Louisville until the next day.

there until the next morning. We were put up in the third story. There were no windows in the window frames, and we could lie on the dirty floor or stand up, as we liked. We couldn't get a civil answer from the guards at the head of the stairs. They used us as though we had been stealing sheep, and we knew they were recruits or one-hundred-day men and hadn't been up at the front. Adam and I went to one of the windows to sit on the window sill. We heard someone holler down in the alley, but didn't think he was hollering at us until he said, "I'll shoot if you don't get back from that window." We told him to shoot if he wanted to, that we had our guns up there and we could shoot too. We told him he had never cocked a cannon, and never had been at the front. He had his gun cocked and at his shoulder when we first saw him, but he took it down when we began talking back. We thought he was bluffing, but when he took his gun down and said he had orders to shoot if we didn't keep back from the windows, we got out of the window. There was a man shot on the other side of the building that afternoon.

There was one soldier who had been in there and was acquainted. He knew we were fresh fish, as they called a newcomer. He told us we had better get close to the door that opened into the dining room so as to get in at the first table or we might not get in at all, as those that got in first would stand near the door and crowd in again at the second table. They served only as many meals as there were guests, and they knew how many men there were in there. Some would go in as many times as they could, just like so many hogs. The grub was a sandwich of bread and fresh boiled beef, and a cup of coffee. The sandwich was on a tin plate. We were let in single file, then marched clear around the table, then stood up and ate the sandwich and drank the tin cup of coffee. Those that were ahead would grab a sandwich off a plate as they passed by, and the the one that came to that place in his turn was out of luck. If he crowded in a second time, someone else would be out his sandwich and would have to wait until the next meal. So we were there at meal time and got our share of grub. We were also ready to go to the train the next morning at nine o'clock, and were the first out for the train.

We were put in a big passenger car, which was new to us. It was an old-style car with no cushions on the seats. But we spread our blankets on the seats and were happy once more. We were still under guard, but didn't care as long as we were going toward our regiment, and we enjoyed the ride across the state of Kentucky to Louisville. We were not allowed to go outside the cars, but we raised the window and bought pies or cake from peddlers outside at the stations where the train stopped. There were plenty of the peddlers, with baskets on their arms, some with pies and some with gingerbread. This was a treat for us. The only place I remember the

name of was Cave City. They told us it was half a mile
to the Mammoth Cave. I would have liked to have seen
it, but that was out of the question.

We got to Louisville that evening and were put in
the guardhouse again. This was a vile-smelling place in
a brick building, but at least there were benches to sit
on. We took a corner near the door. We were taken out
under guard, and marched up the street about a block
and a half, then across the street to what had been the
commons, where they had made a table with a canvas
cover over it, and benches to sit on, with the grub on
the table. We ate our fill. The grub was fine for soldiers
who had been at the front.

We were here two nights and one day; it was a rainy
day too, but the next day was fine, and soon after breakfast we were taken down to the Ohio River, where we
got on a steamboat and went across the river. There we
got on a car again. There was a car full of us from different regiments. We were under a sergeant of the Twelfth
Wisconsin. He was a nice fellow who had seen service
at the front. He said his orders were to put a guard at
each door and not let us out, but that he didn't like to
put a guard over us, and if we would promise we
wouldn't leave him, we might go out as we pleased, but
to be sure not to get left. Adam told him he would
speak for us four, and we wouldn't leave him. All promised the same. When Adam got him alone, he asked him
how we were being sent. He said as combatants return-

ing to our regiment. This was a relief to us, as it was as though we had been in the hospital.

We went through Indiana and into Illinois. I don't remember the names of the towns we went through, but we struck the Illinois Central, and went down it to Cairo, Illinois. If we had gotten there twenty-four hours sooner, we could have gotten a furlough home to vote for the second election of Abraham Lincoln. But we wouldn't have dared to take it. I wasn't old enough to vote anyway, and old Ben Folsom was a Democrat. I don't know what Bill's politics were, but nearly all soldiers were Republicans.

Here at Cairo, we heard our regiment was up at St. Louis, Missouri, so we tried to be sent up there, but the forwarding officer said his orders were to send us to Memphis. So we went down the river to Memphis, Tennessee, where we found a convalescent camp of our regiment. Lieutenant Manley, who we had heard was in the hospital, was there, and many others who had left Worden's Mob. I think we were here about ten days.

One day I took a walk down in the lower part of town. As I was coming back up the street near the river, I heard a man holler, "Oh! Oh!" and saw him come running from a side street about half a block ahead, on the right hand side; and on the far side of the street he turned on the street and came toward me, running as hard as he could, leaning forward as though about to fall, hollering every step, but fainter and fainter until he went out of my sight behind the building on the corner of the street ahead. I hurried forward to see what had happened. There he lay, his head in the open door of a house which looked like a boardinghouse. A policeman got there just as I did. He put his hand on the man's side and said, "He is dead." He wouldn't let anyone come near him.

There was quite a crowd there in a short time, mostly middle-aged women, and all Irish. The policeman said they mustn't touch him until the coroner came. I heard one old lady telling another that he and another man had quarreled about a hammock, and the other had drawn his sheath knife and slashed this one on the neck just below the ear. She said the other had run the other way, turning up the alley near where they were when the deed was done. She saw the quarrel and knew both men, as she called them by their names. They were deck hands on the same steamboat. I didn't stay until the coroner got there as I didn't wish to be mixed up with the sad affair, so went on to camp. I had seen enough of civilian life for one day.

I was detailed for guard one day, and we were put to guard a large pile of government supplies down near the steamboat landing. The pile was covered with a large tarpaulin. It was a dark, cold, rainy night, and I got awfully sleepy. So I got under the tarpaulin to keep dry and warm. I lay my face on a sack of shelled corn and slept the sweet sleep of youth, but woke as I heard the relief coming. There was one of us on each side of the pile. I slept standing up, and felt refreshed when I awoke. I was pleased with myself that I wasn't caught napping.

A few days later we boarded a steamboat and started up the river. The boat stopped at a woodpile to take on wood. Some of the boys went ashore, and one of them pulled an armful of bulrushes. I don't know what he wanted them for, and don't think he knew either. It was just to get something, and I presume he had never seen them before. But I found use for a couple of them when we got to Cairo, Illinois. They were about eighteen inches long, a little bigger than a lead pencil, and hollow and tough.

At Cairo we tied up to a large wharf boat which had a shed built through the middle, and had quite a wide deck around the outside where there were a lot of barrels sitting on end. We would go off on the wharf boat. There were guards every little way, pacing their beats back and forth among the goods. Quite a lot of the boys got off onto the wharf boat, and when tired of walking around, would sit on the barrels. The barrel I sat on was marked sweet cider. How my mouth watered for a drink of that cider.

As the guard didn't object to our sitting on the barrels, I thought of a plan to get a drink. I went up in the boat and inquired around among the boys until I found one who had a gimlet. Then I took two of those bulrushes, cut the top end off, stuck the top of one into the bottom of the other, and put them inside my vest so

I could put the top end in my mouth and the other end into the barrel between my legs. I got on the barrel and when the guard was walking away from me bored a hole with the gimlet, stuck the bulrush down in the barrel, crossed my legs, put the other end in my mouth, and drank cider until I had my fill. There was another man ready to get on as soon as I got off, and there was a man sitting on that barrel until they blew the whistle for "all aboard." It must have been two hours or more, and that cider tasted the best of any I ever drank.

From here, the boat pointed its nose up the Ohio River, and when we got up to the Cumberland River, went up that river to Nashville. Here we left the boat and went into camp a little below the town, where the detachment came to us in a few days. Also, the regiment came from St. Louis, and we were together, except for Company E, which had been detailed to guard the pontoon train, and went with Sherman on his famous march from Atlanta to the sea. I don't think they joined us again until the war ended.

CHAPTER VI

CAMPAIGNING AGAINST HOOD'S ARMY

We had only one commissioned company officer. That was First Lieutenant Jack Manley. One day he took the company over the ridge back of camp and told us he wanted us to elect officers to suit ourselves, as he was going home as soon as his three years were up. We supposed he had re-enlisted, as he went home with us on between-enlistments furlough. So we had an election of officers to fill the vacancies. He said he would recommend those we elected. He took the votes and counted them by himself, or burned them up, and wouldn't tell how the election went. The non-commissioned officers were appointed by the colonel, and the commissioned officers, I think, by the governor of our state on Jack's recommendation.

In a few days he took us over the hill again and gave out the warrants to the sergeants and corporals. Some that had been run for sergeant got corporals' warrants, and one we had voted for as second lieutenant got sergeant warrant. Adam Relyea, who hadn't been run for any office got corporal, and Cy Sturgeon[1] got second

---

[1] Cyrus O. Sturgeon, Neillsville, Clark County. The roster of the company shows Sturgeon as a sergeant; discharged September 22,

lieutenant. He had been in the company a short time the first year, got his discharge, and re-enlisted when we were home on furlough. This caused a good deal of dissatisfaction, and a number of the boys told Jack what they thought of him. They talked awfully mean to him. He tried to shift the blame to the colonel, but the boys weren't deceived.

When Jack's three years were up, he found that he had to serve three years from the date of his commission, and he had to stay with us to the end of the war.[2] This gave me a good deal of satisfaction as well as the others. Mike Crawley was now captain,[3] and Jack didn't have much to say. I know it hurt him as he might have been captain if he had done right.

Adam Relyea wasn't going to accept the office of corporal as he was a recruit and had not been where the bullets flew. He had been in the hospital until the Atlanta campaign was over, and I and others had been in all the battles with the regiment since it left the state. We all urged him to accept it, and he did, and made an excellent corporal. Captain Crawley had me appointed a corporal as soon as there was a vacancy. When Jack got his discharge, he sneaked away without bidding us good-bye, and I never saw him after.

1862, because of disability; re-enlisted January 4, 1864; first sergeant; second lieutenant, February 15, 1865; first lieutenant, June 13, 1865; mustered out October 9, 1865. Houghton, p. 39.

  [2] The record shows he was mustered out May 22, 1865, about five and one-half months before the rest of the company. Houghton, p. 38.

  [3] Crawley became captain December 14, 1864.

Inside a Sutler's Tent

From a pencil and wash drawing by Alfred R. Waud.

The Siege of Vicksburg

The fight in the crater of Fort Hill, after the explosion of
June 25, 1863—General Logan's division and General Mc-
Pherson's corps. From a lithograph of a drawing by A. E.
Mathews.

Going into Bivouac at Night

From a pencil drawing by Edwin Forbes.

Campaigning Against Hood's Army

We built fortifications around Nashville and were ready to receive General Hood, who commanded the Rebs, as soon as he got there. But he didn't charge our works. Instead, he fortified in front of us and waited for us to attack his works. It settled down to picket firing with an occasional artillery bombardment. So we had the same old music we had had all summer. We were on the extreme right, and the Rebs didn't come near enough to us to have any fun with them during the siege.

General Thomas, or "Pap" Thomas, the Rock of Chickamauga, as he was called, was our commander here. As he got ready to go out and attack Hood, a sleet storm came that covered the ground with a coat of ice so thick a man or horse couldn't stand up unless sharp shod. The trees were covered an inch thick with ice. This hung on about ten days and it was awfully cold. But it was worse on the Rebs than on us, as they were not as warmly dressed as we were, and many were barefoot or nearly so. We had only red cedars, and green at that, to make a fire. They made more smoke than fire, so we were glad to see the sun come out and take the ice off. We also knew there would be something doing soon. But we knew it had to come and were anxious to have it over with.

So one morning we were ordered to be ready to march at a moment's notice. We packed up and soon marched outside of our works and off to the right about a mile. Here we formed in line of battle at the edge of the woods, facing an open field and about eighty rods from a stone wall which the Rebs were behind. It was a little uphill to the stone wall and some distance beyond, and there was scattering timber back of that. It wasn't at all a good-looking place to make a charge and all were quiet. There was no laughing or joking. It showed all were busy with their thoughts.

Brigadier General Ward had been our colonel ever since the Battle of Shiloh, and had been promoted to general a short time before. All the boys admired him. I have said General Ward, but I don't think he had his commission at this time, but was in command of the brigade. He was riding a brown horse which he had ridden for over two years. It was sleek and fat. We all liked Ward as he was always good to us, and was a nice-appearing man on a horse. He was not more than two rods in front of me, and as cool appearing as if we were on drill. As he faced us, he said, "Boys, now take it easy and follow me. I will lead you." As he gave the command, saying, "Right shoulder, shift arms, forward, double quick, march," he wheeled his horse around and we were off for the stone wall, the whole brigade in line.

I know his appearance helped me, and I think it did the whole command, to keep cool and not get excited. We were not to cheer as we would in a charge, but we knew the Rebs were behind the wall. We saw puffs of smoke at the top of the wall, but their bullets went over us. When we were a little more than halfway to the wall, we saw a strong skirmish line leave the stone wall and go back at a lively run. This pleased me, and I think it did the rest of the command. But when we were about fifteen rods from the wall, about as many more Rebs jumped over the wall without their guns and came to meet us. One I saw was cutting his belt off with his pocket knife and laughing. I saw him cut his finger, then he stopped laughing and looked at what he was doing.

George King,[4] who had come to the company the night before and had never been on drill, was at the left of the company. When he saw the Rebs coming toward us, he raised his gun to his shoulder to shoot at them. But the man next to him wouldn't let him shoot. George said, "How do you expect to put down the rebellion if you don't shoot the sons-of-bitches when you have a chance?"[5] When the man was telling us about it, George looked sheepish and didn't laugh with the rest of us.

There was a gun battery that belonged to the brigade. It was just to the left of our regiment and the regiment to our left. They went forward with us, and all went over the stone wall together. When we reached the top of the slope, where we halted, they unlimbered and be-

[4] George R. King, Neillsville, Clark County, enlisted September 3, 1864; mustered out October 9, 1865. He, too, was only fifteen at the time he enlisted, and had tried to enlist several times before being accepted. Houghton, p. 48.
[5] Edgar P. Houghton, in his "History of Company I" (p. 48), relates this same story.

gan to throw shells after the fleeing Rebs, who were going into the timber on the other side of the open field. It was surprising the way those artillerymen handled those guns. There were six horses on a gun. They had to turn around before they unhitched, and it looked as if they were all getting mixed up, but the four guns were dropped at the same time, and the horses in a dead run went to the rear some rods where they took another switch and faced the guns, which were firing ball by this time at the fleeing Rebs. It was surprising how fast they could shoot those cannon. A shell would hardly get over to the woods before another from the same gun was on the way over there. This was music to our ears, as we knew it was unpleasant for the Rebs. We hoped they wouldn't stop on the other side, and they didn't. But those guns soon got so hot they had to stop shooting and let them cool off.

While we were getting our wind, Wm. Hutchenson,[6] our company clerk who had followed us, came up. He didn't have to carry a gun, only the company books in his haversack. We had passed through a small graveyard after passing the stone wall. One grave was fenced with a picket fence, and weeds and grass had grown up inside. He stopped to look in and saw a Reb with his gun hid in the weeds. He told the Reb to give him the gun. The Reb readily gave up the gun and belts, and Billy came to us smiling, as was also the Reb. The Reb said

[6] William T. Hutchenson, Neillsville, Clark County, enlisted November 7, 1861; mustered out October 9, 1865. Houghton, p. 40.

he had hid there thinking we wouldn't see him, and as soon as we were out of sight, he was going home, since he lived not far from there and hadn't been home for two years, and had had all the fighting he wanted. Some of these prisoners were barefoot and some with their toes sticking out of their shoes. All their clothes were threadbare, and as dirty as we had been in the Atlanta campaign.

When we had rested, we went forward again. This time there was a line of skirmishers ahead of us. We went about a mile. Where we halted we heard heavy firing to the left and some musketry. Some distance to the right we saw a brigade charge up quite a steep hill where the Rebs had a strong line of breastworks. But our boys went over the hill out of sight. Near sundown the firing quieted down to picket firing in the distance. We made our coffee and lay down to sleep. We hadn't lost a man in our regiment, but it had been quite exciting all day. General Hood had sacrificed his command but hadn't whipped the Army of the Tennessee, as he had said he would when he took command some five months before. He had suffered a bad repulse at Franklin before reaching Nashville, where he lost heavily. One of his best generals had also been killed there, General Pat Cleburne.

The next morning about ten o'clock we marched after the fleeing Rebs. We met several squads of prisoners coming back. I suppose they had been picked up by our cavalry. We were on a macadamized road made of broken rock. This was hard on our shoes. It had rained during the night and the mud and water were shoe deep in places. My shoes were a little short, and I hadn't trimmed my toenails, so my big toenails hit against the end of my shoes. They hurt me all day, but I didn't think enough to amount to anything. When I took my shoes off though, my toenails were black. The blood had settled under them, and they were pretty sore on the rest of that march. I trimmed them down as short as I could and they went pretty good the next day.

We didn't come up with the Rebs until we got to Duck River, where they had burned the bridge. Here the advance had a little skirmish with their rear guard, and the battery threw over a few shell, and they took to the woods again. We got across the river that evening. The next day they told us we would lay there. It was Christmas.

Ed Markey heard that an Irishman lived about fifteen miles from there who had all kinds of liquor in his cellar. He said if Charley King and I would go with him, we would go and get some for Christmas. So we went about eight miles and inquired of some darkies, who told us he lived fifteen miles farther on. We decided not to look for that Irishman any more, and looked for something at this place.

There was a small building sided with narrow slats. We could see several beehives inside. These hives were the old-style hives, but had wire screen tacked over the

openings so the bees couldn't get out. The door had a
padlock on it. Also, a hound was chained up in there.
King said if we could get one of those hives out we
could get some honey. But he didn't like the looks of
that dog. I told him we weren't afraid of a hound, especially when she was chained up, but that Ed and I didn't
want anything to do with bees. He said if we would
get one of the hives out of there, he would get the honey
out. So Ed got a couple of stones and broke the padlock,
set the hive out on the ground, and got back out of the
way to see him get the honey. He took one of the stones
and knocked the top off the hive, and with his two
hands broke the honey down so the bees couldn't get
out, and said, "Boys, come on," as he took a nice piece
of honey and began eating it. Ed and I went up, as we
didn't see any bees. It was nice, white honey, free from
brood or bee bread.

As we were eating, the man that owned the place
came, and complained because we had broken his padlock. Ed told him if he had things locked up, he had
better be around with the key when we came around,
if he didn't want the lock broken, as we had to have
something to eat, and as it was Christmas, we wanted
something extra. He said he had locked that door because he didn't want dogs to get in to that she hound.
Ed squared up to him and told him not to call us dogs.

He said, "No, I don't mean that, but I don't want
dogs to get in."

Ed said, "You can whittle out a stick to put in the

staple. It will keep the dogs out as well as the padlock."

We kept on eating honey and the fellow left us. When we had our fill, King went down to the Negro quarters and borrowed a brass kettle that would hold a good pail full. The old Negro didn't like to let the kettle go, but Charley told him he would fetch it back tomorrow. But tomorrow never came—didn't in that case. We filled the kettle with nice comb honey, got a pole, and strung the kettle on it so we could carry it on our shoulders. It was too heavy to carry that far in our hands.

On the way back we stopped at another big plantation where there was a large smokehouse. There were a lot of nice-looking hams and lots of bacon hanging up. There was also a big trough that had been dug out of a log. It was full of meat in salt before being smoked. We took the biggest smoked ham we saw, and King got a stick so he could carry it on his shoulder. When we got a little way from there, Ed and I began to have the stomachache, and soon we both bloated so we could hardly breathe. We had to stop every little way to rest. Then King would take another piece of honey and say, "Boys, eat some more. What will kill will cure." But we had had enough, and for years after the thought of honey made me sick. I suffered all night and had the "Tennessee quick step" as the boys used to call chronic diarrhea. I never tasted that ham either. It didn't hurt King nor any of the rest of the boys, who made short work of both the honey and the ham.

The next day we resumed the march. One day on this march we were pretty near the advance, and we should have drawn rations that morning, but the teams were behind, so we had to go without. A cold drizzly rain set in and kept up nearly all day. About noon we stopped to rest. There was a house a little way ahead, and Adam went up there. There was a big kettle near the house. It had been full of fat pork they were trying out for lard. But other soldiers were ahead of him and one of them just fished out the last piece as he got there. Adam gave the fellow fifty cents for a part of it. He cut it into four equal pieces and gave Bill, Ben, and me a piece, and ate the other himself. There was a good big mouthful apiece. He said that before he left home he wouldn't have eaten that mouthful for a five-dollar bill. But it was the sweetest mouthful I ever ate.

That night we camped in a piece of timber near the road. Across a swale there was a small field. Over there I saw a lot of boys from the regiment ahead, so I went over. It was small flat turnips they were after. I pulled turnips as long as there was one left, and got about all I could carry in my arm. I took them over to camp, threw them down beside a log, and told the boys to help themselves. I sat on the log and went to peeling and eating.

The boys said, "Lish, they will kill you."

I said, "I might as well die eating turnips as starve to death," and ate my fill. They didn't hurt me.

Everyone wanted a fire. The wood was green and

wet and made more smoke than fire. The smoke settled to the ground, and the woods was soon full of smoke, and all were crying. We put up our tent and I got in. I had a small piece of salt pork I had carried in my haversack for a long time with the hope we would get some fresh meat I could fry with it. I decided to eat that and got it out. It was as black as tar on the outside, and yellow on the inside. It was so rancid, I ate a little, but couldn't go it and threw it away, then curled up in my blankets to get rid of the awful smoke that was almost stifling, and slept until morning.

The teams caught up late that night, and we drew rations the next morning. The doctor ordered a jigger of whiskey, and those that were supposed to be good judges said it was pure whiskey but needed ageing in wood barrels two or three years, after which it would be slick and smooth. A jigger was a gill, and one was all I could carry at once, and more than I wanted. Adam and Ben wouldn't drink the stuff at all but when in camp used it to wash their heads. We had no bottle to carry it in and were talking about what to do with it, and had decided to throw it away.

Bill had drunk his and said, "Don't throw it away. If you don't want it, I will drink it." I gave him my cup. He downed it and smacked his lips. Adam gave him his, then Ben, and he smacked his lips each drink, and looked pleased.

I said, "You won't march today."

"Yes, I will," he said, "that is nothing. I could drink

as much more and then march." He said he had worked in a distillery and drank nothing but whiskey. If I hadn't seen him drink it, I wouldn't have known he had drunk any. So after that we knew what to do with our jiggers. We didn't draw whiskey regularly, only when the doctor ordered it.

The soles of my shoes were going out, and we had no more with us and couldn't draw new ones. The soles soon wore off back to the hollow of my foot. When the uppers chafed the tops of my toes, I would cut a piece off. Then it would chafe a little higher up. My feet were getting as sore on top as they were on the bottoms, and I finally threw the shoes away and went barefoot until I could draw new ones, which was some weeks later. We had gotten off the macadamized road and were on a gravel road. This seemed much better for bare feet, and I got along fine that day. But I found out when I got to camp there was a blood blister on the bottom of each toe, and the balls of my feet just back of the toes were also blistered. But they didn't hurt me that night and I slept well.

It was late when we got to camp, so we did not put up our tents, but made our beds on the ground, and spread pieces of tent over us, covered up head and ears and slept nice and warm. We were surprised the next morning to find about four inches of snow on top of us. It was cold snow, too, with a slight crust on top, and it didn't feel good to my bare feet. But we had to get out early as we were on the advance this day. This was

New Year's morn, 1865. My feet were so sore and I was out of humor and too ugly to be decent. When we fell in to march, I took my place in the rear rank.

Ed Houghton came along behind me and stopped and said, "Gosh, Lish, I wouldn't start like that."

I said, "What would you do?"

He said, "I would cut my blanket up and tie it on my feet."

I said, "Do you think I'm a damn fool?" and he passed on without any reply. I was ashamed for saying what I had, for I knew he was sorry to see me in that snow. But I was too ugly at the time and didn't want any sympathy. Years after, he would tell about it at our reunions, and then he claimed I said, "Them feet belong to Uncle Sam and if he don't furnish shoes to put on 'em, let 'em freeze."

I was detached for advance guard, so could get out to one side of the road. The blisters broke and blood dyed the snow and made it look worse than it really was. It was bad enough to suit me anyway. But after going a mile or two, they didn't hurt me. They weren't cold, but fairly burned. By noon the snow was all gone. We went into camp early. Those in advance would camp about three o'clock or as soon after as a good camping ground was reached. Then the rear would be after dark getting in.

This country was fairly level. That is, there were no big hills, but rolling, some small hills, and mostly covered with timber, all hardwood, but not much underbrush. It was very thickly settled. What houses there were in sight of the road were mostly well back from the road. The soil was red clay, the reddest I ever saw.

After we got to camp that day King, Mose Fuller, and Adam Relyea went out and got a big, nice sheep, and we had mutton for supper, breakfast, and dinner the next day. My feet hurt me so I couldn't sleep, so I got up and roasted mutton until I had it all roasted. There were six of us in on the sheep, and we finished it for dinner. This was the only fresh meat we got on this march. The Rebs kept it cleaned up ahead of us, and I suppose told the citizens we were coming, and they drove what the Rebs didn't take well back from the road until we had passed.

The next day we were to be toward the rear so would be late to camp. I went to the doctor with my feet, which were pretty sore. He said the wagons and ambulances were loaded to the limit. There were others barefoot, and more were sick, but he said he would excuse me from duty and I could start with the advance and have all day to make it to camp. I told him that was good, but I said, "There is my gun and belts. I won't carry them any further." He said he would try and get them on the wagons, and he did. I made it quite easy. We only marched about fifteen miles a day, and one could make it much easier by himself than he could in the ranks.

We camped some two miles from the Tennessee River. There was a small town here, I think it was Clifton, Tennessee. The Rebs had gotten across the river. They had split up when they left Nashville and taken several roads. They had captured a steamboat which had ferried them across the river. We lay here several days. The old chronic diarrhea came back on me and, with my sore feet, made it unpleasant for me. So I stayed in the tent pretty close. When the boats came up, they took us aboard. I rode in the ambulance down to the boat. This was the first time I had ridden in an ambulance.

We went up the river past Savannah, and Pittsburg Landing, and Hamburg, Tennessee. These were familiar places to me, but we did not stop at any of these places. We went up to Eastport, Mississippi, where we went into winter quarters of our own making. The boats had brought plenty of corn for the mules, but nothing but coffee, bacon, sugar, and salt for us—not even a pair of shoes. I have said that a person wasn't supposed to know any more than the mules, and was not thought as much of as the mules. This was proof of it. So we had to borrow corn from the mules for about ten days.

We camped on a high bluff overlooking the river. There were only a few trees on it, and the boys had to go down in a ravine to get wood and timber to build our shacks. Most of them just put up their tents, but Adam and Bill built us a log house and covered it with pieces of our tents. I don't remember the size of it, but I think it was about seven feet square. They built bunks one above the other on the back side, a fireplace in one corner, and a door in the other corner on the front side. They got small logs and split them, notched the corners together, with the split side in, and hewed the inside after getting it laid up, then covered it with the tent pieces, and mudded it up on the outside. The fireplace was built of stone and mud part way up, and split sticks and mud the rest of the way. We hung a blanket up for a door, and it was nice and warm inside. The boys wouldn't let me help with the shebang, so all I could do was parch the corn, make the coffee, fry the bacon, and warm my toes.

The mules were camped down on the flat near the river and we could look down on them. The mornings were cold and frosty and still. About sunrise they would begin feeding them, and they would set up an awful din, several thousand of them all braying at once. When they were fed their corn, all would be quiet. One morning George Hill of Company D was out looking down on them, and as soon as they were quiet, he began braying. He could bray equal to any mule. Soon there were several hundred helping him, and the rest were laughing at them bray for their corn.

The first ration we drew after the corn was a pound of flour to each man. We had no way to cook it but to stir it up with water and fry it with bacon grease. I told the boys (there were four of us in our mess) that I was going to make bread of my share, but that I would cook theirs as they wanted it, and that it would take all day to make bread. Adam and Bill said to cook theirs with mine. But Ben didn't see how I could make bread with just water, salt, and flour. I said, "I can if I don't have bad luck, but will make pancakes of your share if you say so." But he said, "The majority rules, so make mine with the rest." I asked Adam if he would hunt up a skillet to bake it in, and said I would start my end of things at once. I told him if he could get some soda or baking powder I would make some biscuits. He got a skillet from the headquarters cook, but couldn't get soda or baking powder. So I made the bread, and it took me until near midnight.

The boys were fast asleep when I got it done, so I rolled it up in a clean towel and put it away in a little cupboard Adam had made out of a cracker box, and went to bed with Adam. Ben had grumbled some before going to bed; said if we had made pancakes as the others did, we would have had something. So the next morning they asked how I came out with my bread. I said I had spoiled it. "That's just what I expected," said Ben. So I fetched out the loaf, and they all called it the best bread they ever ate. We ate the whole of it for breakfast with coffee and bacon. It was the best bread I ever ate.

We drew hardtack after this while we were here, and I got shoes. The reason we were so long on corn was because the ice was so thick in the river that the boats could hardly make headway against it. Nearly half the paddles were broken out of the wheels.

Union Picket Post near Atlanta

The Union Line before Nashville

One day we got marching orders. We packed up, some tearing down their chimneys so they wouldn't be of any use to the Rebs if they should come that way. We left ours stand and just took off our tent. We went from here to Iuka the first day, and to Corinth, Mississippi, the next day. We stopped about a mile from Corinth, and other regiments went to the town. That was about two o'clock in the afternoon and it was about four o'clock when we left. There was only one nice building there. It was called the Tishomingo Hotel. It was a large three-story frame building near the depot, and a junction. That hotel was all afire before we started back. We heard the Rebs had been quartered there.

We were only a small command. I think just our brigade. We went back the way we had come. It was dark soon after we started back, and they gave orders not to talk loud, but to keep as quiet as possible. So we knew our officers were afraid of being cut off from the rest of the command. It was dark and the road was rough, there being small stumps and some mud puddles. We hadn't had our coffee, were tired, and many were cross at the way they were hurrying us along. Some would stub their toes on a stump and would swear so loud they could be heard quite a distance. Finally Charley Stahl went sprawling in a mud puddle. When he got up, the air was blue around him, and he shot his gun off as he had got it full of water. He swore he would shoot an officer if one came back there. An officer soon came back, probably an aid of the commander.

He wanted to know who fired that shot. But before anyone could answer, someone fired his gun over his horse's tail. Then four or five more shots were fired a little farther back. It was so dark he couldn't see who they were, so he put spurs to his horse and went back to the front.

I didn't like this, as it was mutiny. The whole regiment could be put under arrest if we didn't tell who did the shooting, and if we told on them, they would be punished severely. I didn't like being marched as hard as we were, but the officers knew better than we why we were running so. It was necessary to have discipline, and I feared there would be trouble over this. But soon Colonel Ward, who was in command of the brigade came back. He said, "Boys, be quiet. We will soon be to camp." And all were quiet. He spoke in a quiet tone as though nothing serious had happened, but in a decisive tone. I could have hugged him for it. It was just such acts as this that made the men all like him. We heard no more about it, and some two or three miles farther we reached camp at Iuka where we had left that morning. I don't remember just how far it is, but it was over thirty miles we had marched that day.[7]

I was detailed for picket duty, and we went about a mile back on the road we had come on. I was posted on the left side of the road some forty or fifty rods from

[7] Present-day highway maps show Corinth to be twenty-two miles from Iuka. Thus they evidently marched at least forty-four miles that day besides spending the two hours in Corinth.

the road. The road was on a high ridge that was covered with big timber. I was about halfway down the hill beside a big tree. I had no water to make coffee, and I thought if I stood here two hours, then went to get water, it would be near morning by the time I got my supper, so I wouldn't get any sleep. I felt sure we would march early that morning. The moon had gotten so it was light, and I could see there was a deep ravine below. I thought there would be water holes down there, so I set my gun up beside the tree so I could find the same tree when I came back. I followed that ravine half a mile or more before I found water. I filled my canteen and the little pail I made coffee in and hurried back. I couldn't find my gun, and after hunting some time made up my mind I wouldn't be caught there without a gun and would go to camp and get one. I started for camp, but didn't get far when there before me sat my gun. I had been looking too far up the ravine. I was a tickled boy and vowed never to leave my post again without my gun. I went up to the rear and soon had made my coffee, eaten my supper, and was in the land of dreams.

As soon as daylight brightened the east, we went back to camp, where we found all up getting ready for the march. Soon after noon we were back at our camp at Eastport, where we had left three days before. All we had to do was put the roof on our house, hang up the blanket in the door, and we were at home. Those that had torn theirs down had to work all the next day fixing them up.

Soon after this there was a camp rumor that we were going to march down through Mississippi and Alabama to the Gulf, and that they would have a big supply train. A few days later there was a call for volunteers to drive mules. The marching had been so hard the past summer, I thought I would try skinning mules, as the boys used to call mule driving. There was quite a bunch of us, and we were taken down on the flat where the teams were camped. There was a big pile of pieces of old harnesses, all well worn. They told us to put our harnesses together. I was suspicious at once—thought I could see the tail of a very small mouse! So I with several others sat down and looked on while the rest scrambled and clawed the pile of old straps over, each trying to get the best pieces for his harness. The wagon master came and told us if we wanted to drive mules we had better get to work and get our harness together. But we told him, "Let them fellows have their pick and we will take what is left." He didn't urge us any more.

When they got their harness together, they went down where the mules were. When I saw the mules, I was glad I hadn't put any harness together, and if I had, I wouldn't have put it on those mule skins. But there was another scramble for the best-looking mules. When all were harnessed, they were told to hitch onto those old wagons. They then loaded what was left of the old straps into the wagons and drove up to headquarters. Here the whole was turned over to the ordnance department, and we were told to report back to our companies until called for. I thought us privates didn't know nearly as much as the mules, for they did know how to kick, kick good and hard, when they were imposed upon. This was the last of our mule driving. One of the boys in my company asked me why I didn't tell him it was a fake. I said I didn't know it was a fake, but I did know that if I was going to drive mules, I wasn't going to start out with an old worn-out outfit like that was.

CHAPTER VII

THE GULF CAMPAIGN

A few days later there was a whole string of steamboats came up the river and both banks were lined with them, all empty. So we concluded we were going to have a boat ride, where to, we had no idea and cared less. It would beat marching anyway. We did get a good long ride—to New Orleans.

As we passed Pittsburg Landing there was a single musket shot fired at our boat from the top of the hill above the landing. No one lived there. It was only a steamboat landing, as also was Hamburg and Eastport above it. But Savannah, twelve miles below Pittsburg, was quite a little village.

We went down the Tennessee to the Ohio River, then down to the Mississippi, and on down to New Orleans. We were on the upper or hurricane deck. The weather was fine and we enjoyed this ride. One day I was sitting near the railing that went around the outside of the deck, reading a novel, when there were several shots fired at us from the east shore of the river. The Rebs were behind the levee with just their heads above, and they had a brass cannon at the edge of the woods. We scrambled for the other side of the boat, and some of the boys who had their guns loaded took a shot at them. They ran for the woods a few rods away. The boat behind us had some artillery on it and threw a shell over in the woods. This was all the excitement we had on the trip.

The boats kept from a half-mile to a mile apart, and often we would see the boats that were half an hour ahead of us going back nearly north the way we had come, the river was so crooked in places. It didn't look more than eighty rods across in places. The country looked lower than the river as far as we could see. The timber was bare of leaves, with a gray moss hanging from the limbs, which made the trees look as if they were dead. The country looked forsaken as we couldn't see the houses if a few rods back from the river.

From Baton Rouge down, it looked better as there were houses on both sides of the river and orange trees loaded with oranges. These were the first orange trees the most of us had ever seen, and it was a grand sight. We were crazy to get ashore, as we were tired of riding anyway. So when the boat turned its nose toward the shore and the deck hands began to shove out the gangplank, all was excitement on the lower deck. As soon as the bow touched the shore, a lot of the boys jumped, not waiting for them to get the gangplank out. We on the upper deck were envious of those on the lower deck as there were orange trees on the top of the levee loaded with nice big oranges. But I saw one man bite into the first one he got hold of, and he dropped it like it had been a hot potato. He looked around to see if anyone was looking at him and saw us laughing. He shook his head at us and went farther up the levee. We knew something was wrong, but the other boys were scrambling for the nicest-looking ones and cramming their pockets full before they tasted of them. But they were more sour than lemons, and when one would taste of them, he would try to hide it. But soon one got a bite who was so disgusted that he swore like a pirate.

I think it was on this trip that there was a total eclipse of the sun, the only one I ever saw. It was about noon. There was not a cloud in the sky, and the first thing we knew it began to get dark. When we looked up at the sun, it looked like a new moon—about the first quarter. When the eclipse was full, there was a small ring, just enough to see where the sun was. It was so dark we couldn't see each other enough to tell who anyone was a few feet away. It was uncanny, and made one feel as though he had gotten into another world. Everybody was quiet, all looking up at the sun as if it might go out entirely. It had been shining so brightly so short a time before. And now it was so dark. I can't express the feeling I had, and I thought, what would we do if it disappeared entirely? When it came out from the shadow, it seemed brighter than ever before.

I saw another eclipse, I think it was in 1869. I and another man were carrying hay off a boggy marsh, and it got so dark we couldn't see the bogs so had to sit down until the sun came out. But there was only about seven-eighths of the sun covered this time. My wife had to light the lamp to see to work though, and said the chickens went to roost.

We went into camp a little below New Orleans on General Jackson's old battlefield where the Battle of New Orleans was fought in the War of 1812. It had been used for truck gardening. It was a dead-level piece of land with ditches every few rods square for the water to settle away. It was, I should guess, fourteen feet lower than the Mississippi River. It rained several days while we were here, and the ditches were full of water for a week. We had our pup tents staked to the ground so had to lay on the ground. Our tent was close to a ditch, and one morning there was a dead lizard in Adam's and my bed. We had lain on it and killed it. It was about a foot long, and it made the cold chills run up and down my back when I saw it.

One day we discovered a water snake about three feet long in the hay we had for our bed. Adam struck at it with the axe as it ran into the ditch. He said he knew he hit it, but it got into the ditch. When the water settled away, there it was dead, curled around some roots. He had cut it nearly in two. This was not pleasant to think about when we went to bed, but we would stir up the hay before lying down at night. I didn't like the snake, but preferred snakes to the lizard.

There was a monument a little way from camp to commemorate the battle.[1] It was built of brick. It was

---

[1] Battle of New Orleans in the War of 1812.

round, about twelve feet across at the ground, and I don't remember how high, but it was over one hundred feet. An iron stair inside wound to the top. It was a sightly place at the top. The monument wasn't finished, and there were a lot of bricks around there. Some boys in another company got some of them and built a Dutch oven of them, using mud for mortar. There was lots of that ready mixed. It was shoe deep all over the camp. The oven was a fine success. One could bake anything in it fine. We cut up our hardtack with our jackknives, soaked it overnight in cold water sweetened with sugar, and seasoned with allspice and cinnamon, and baked it in the oven. It was like a bread pudding, but better than any pudding I ever ate.

The weather cleared up and the mud dried up so life was worth living once more, and one nice day I took a walk in the country east of camp. It was all truck gardening as far as I went, or rather had been. I went some two or three miles before seeing a house. There was a house and a little back of it was a fine-looking garden. I saw five or six soldiers coming toward it from the other side. A very large young woman came out of the house with her sleeves rolled up above her elbows. She swore like a man and called those soldiers nigger thieves, and said if they touched those vegetables she would come over there. They laughed at her and told her they didn't want her truck. But she kept on with slang, and told them to come up there two at a time and she would lick the whole bunch. I thought I had seen enough and turned back toward camp. I heard later that she was a French Creole.

When we left here we marched up through the city, past the statue of General Jackson on his horse, out by the race course and fair grounds, and struck a road running east to Lake Pontchartrain. The road led straight through low, swampy country to the lake. There was timber all the way, and a big part of the road was covered with logs or poles. I don't remember that we saw a house all the way. I think it was some twelve miles. We got on a boat here, a large side-wheel steamer that had been made for the lower Mississippi River. There were two decks, and we were on the upper one. It had a large walking beam that turned the wheels to propel the boat. It was a clumsy-looking boat.

We went down the lake to the Gulf and around the Gulf to Dauphin Island off the mouth of Mobile Bay. This was the first time I had been on salt water and out of sight of land. It was a nice still day, but the whitecaps were rolling, and it looked plenty rough enough to suit the most of us, especially with that old tub of a boat. The sea gulls were following close behind, and the porpoises were rolling on both sides of us. The old men who had been on the ocean said that portended a storm, and we were glad to get off on the island.

The island looked embarrassingly small. It was out of sight of the mainland. There was a sand island a little way east of it that had a fort with big guns on it. That was at the entrance to Mobile Bay for big boats. Dauphin Island was covered with timber, but thinly, and with no underbrush. It was a nice place to camp, and we enjoyed our stay here, which was some two weeks. On a clear day we could see a dark line to the north. It was said to be the mainland, and it was said one could wade ashore when it was low tide and no wind.

One day three of us waded out nearly half a mile to fish for oysters. We had gunnysacks to carry our oysters in. We could feel them with our feet. When we felt one, we would reach down with our hand and get it. Sometimes it would be a stone, but not often. The water most of the way was up to our knees, and in some places up to our necks for a few steps. There was one place that it was up to our arms for about twenty feet. This was about a third of the way out. We just had our shoes on and were otherwise naked.

The tide had begun to come in when we saw a small black cloud coming up over to the back of the island. So we started for the island as fast as we could go. We thought we would leave the oysters so we could go faster, but I hated to give up the oysters. We had about a bushel each. We soon came to one of the deep places, and I saw it would be hard to keep on the bottom if I didn't have the oysters to hold me down, so we stuck to the sacks of oysters. The squall came fast and met us before we were halfway back. There were quite large waves or big riffles that would lift us off our feet, so it was hard work to make headway. There was also quite a current by this time, and where the water had been up to our knees, it was up to our hips; where it had been up to our arms, it was over our heads, and we had to duck under and hold our breath until we got across where we could get our heads out. I saw we could make better time under the water than on top, so where the water was deep I would duck under as long as I could hold my breath, and the other boys did the same.

The water was getting deeper very fast, but as we got nearer the island, it got smoother on top, and the current was not so strong. But the tide was rising fast, and quite a way before we got ashore it was up to our necks. Some of the boys came to meet us and help us. They thought we could never make it alone. We were nearly all in when we got ashore, and we lay on the sand some little time to get rested before we put our clothes on. We had had all the oyster fishing we wanted for a lifetime.

The boys on shore had a good fire, and the storm had passed and the sun shone again, and we had a good oyster feast. We opened them by laying them on the coals. Then they would open themselves, and we would put salt, pepper and a few drops of vinegar on them and eat them out of the shell. There was quite a crowd of our boys there, but we had enough for all.

Just before we left New Orleans quite a squad of drafted men had been sent to us from the state,[2] and

---

[2] Apparently Wisconsin. Edgar P. Houghton, who obviously had records available, says the company received twenty-four recruits brought out by the draft in January, 1865. Houghton, p. 44.

about fifteen of them were assigned to our company and they had to drill. So every day the awkward squad, as they were called, had to drill while we were here on the island, but there wasn't room to have company or regiment drill. So we had no duty to perform and had to pass the time as best we could. We played cards, marbles, pull sticks, run and jump, or stand and jump, wrestled, boxed, or played shake hands. I was good at hardly any of these, but could shake hands with any of them. This required a good grip. I could pull fingers pretty well, but at pulling sticks was no good, as those who were lighter than I was could pull me up.

There was an Irishman by the name of Richard Johnson among the drafted men. He was a rank Reb to hear him talk. He said he would shoot high enough to shoot over them if he got where he had to shoot. He said he thought we had no right to make them stay in the Union. Some of the boys would argue with him for hours and call him a Rebel, and ask him why he hadn't gone down and enlisted with the Rebs if he thought they were right. But he would laugh and take any abuse they gave him. He made a good soldier and was one of the first ones to apply for a pension after getting home. He was a good fellow. I think he talked for the sake of an argument.

When we left here, we landed quite a way east of Mobile Bay and marched up to Spanish Fort on Mobile Bay.[3] This was a strong fort and one could see that it would be hard to take by storm. It was on a sandy level plain. The timber had been cut off for three-quarters of a mile back from the fort. They had used the tops of the trees to make entanglements, by cutting the ends of the limbs off where they were about two inches through and sharpening them with a drawing knife, and taking the bark off so they couldn't be easily set on fire. They were laid some eight rods from the fort and were about twenty feet wide clear around it. There was a road through this for their convenience, but guns in the fort commanded this. Outside this entanglement they had what we called sheep racks. They were made of the longest logs they could get. Holes had been bored through the logs each way and then sticks driven halfway through and sharpened at both ends, so if it was rolled over, it was the same as on the other side.

There was a low ridge about three-quarters of a mile from the fort. We camped back of it. There was scattering timber on the ridges and back of it. It was a nice place to camp, but the Rebs put a big gun on a sand island out in the bay. It threw a 175-pound shell, and it enfiladed our line. The shell was sure to land somewhere along the line, and they made it disagreeable for us for several days. Only one man was hurt in our regiment, but a regiment to the right of us had one company nearly annihilated by one of those shells. We could see it coming but couldn't tell where the darned thing was going to light. Some would go clear over, and some

<hr />

[3] March 27, 1865, according to General Grant, having been at Dauphin Island since March 12, 1865. *Personal Memoirs*, II, 519.

would light before they got to us. We could run several rods while it was coming. But it always looked like it was coming right where you were, so those that were down at the foot of the hill ran up hill, and those up the hill ran down. Everyone moved and all were excited until it had hit, when we would quiet down until the next one was on the way.

We had built breastworks at the top of the slope to protect us from shells from the fort, and now each company built a short one to protect us from the pieces of shell from the sand island gun, whose shells sometimes burst before getting to us. We had just gotten this trench finished when I saw that someone had set a gun against our tent. It was against the tent so I got out of the ditch to take the gun off. I was reaching for the gun when several hollered, "Look out." I looked up the hill as I had heard the explosion that way, and I saw a piece of shell coming over the hill. I jumped back into the ditch and it made a hole through the edge of the tent. It would have made a hole through me if I hadn't gotten out of the way just as I did. It struck the ground and bounded. The sergeant-major sat about four rods down the hill eating his supper. His back was toward us. The piece of shell went over his right shoulder, ticked his right temple and knocked him over. But he got up, thankful that it wasn't any worse. This had come from the fort. It was a piece of percussion shell that had burst over the hill.

The next morning the Company D cook had just

brought the company's coffee and was dealing it out to the men. I was a few rods from them and looking at them. They were all around the coffee pot when a shell came from the fort and smashed that kettle flat, sprinkled the whole bunch with coffee, went about eight rods farther, and went in the ground without touching a man. It looked like an impossibility for it to get through that crowd without touching anyone.

There was only part of the command here. The other part had gone farther up the bay and laid siege to Fort Blakely. General Canby was in command of both. I never heard who commanded the Rebels.

We dug a trench across that sand plain. It was zig-zag like a worm fence. We dug it in the night, just wide enough to work in, throwing the dirt out on the side facing the fort. Then we dug this wider so we could haul cannon out there. It was moonlight nights when we commenced this. They strung us along where they wanted the road. Two went to one shovel, and the men were as thick as they could be. We shoveled hard. When one tired, the other would take the shovel while he lay down on the ground near by, on the side opposite that on which the dirt was being thrown out. It was sandy enough so it was easy shoveling, but the Rebs could see the bright shovels glisten in the moonlight, and they would fire a volley at us. Then we would hug the ground, or if in the ditch would huge the bottom of that. We were ordered not to talk out loud, and those that were resting were to get behind a log or stump when one was near. These orders were obeyed, especially after the Rebs had fired the first volley at us.

This was the first time those drafted men had heard minnie [Minié] bullets whistle, but they stood it fine. One, a German, was lying behind a small log while the Rebs were firing. They kept at it some time. The German was saying his prayers just above a whisper when a bullet struck the other side of the log. That German rolled for the ditch which was about eight feet away. It took him about as long to get to that ditch as it does for me to tell it. He rolled kerplunk on top of the man in the ditch, but there wasn't any fault found by the other fellow. There was no shirking on this job either. Everyone wanted to shovel all the time, for the one resting would get cold and want to warm up.

We got these roads dug so we could get out to the rifle pits in the daytime. Then if one got wounded or killed, he could be taken back and not have to lay there until night. Then we built a fort for our four cannon and hauled them out by hand, and the Rebs quit throwing shells over to our camp. We brought up two big guns off a gunboat and the Jackies came with them to operate them. They were set a little way to the left of our regiment. I think they were one-hundred-pounders, but the Rebs would repair the damage during nights that had been done through the day.

The sand-bar gun quit annoying us as did the cannon in the fort. But they got a small mortar that threw a twelve-pound shell, and one day when my company was in the trenches they made it very disagreeable for us. They would toss those shells up in the air, and they would come overhead and burst, and the pieces would scatter every way. All we could do was hug up against the breastworks. Fred Mattice[4] wouldn't hug the dirt and would laugh at us. But finally he got a piece on his head, and three days later he died. He never became conscious, just lay there and moaned. This cast a gloom over the company, as he was liked by all who knew him. He had left the state with us and had been through all the battles that the regiment had taken part in. He had never received a scratch nor missed a turn of duty, and he left four motherless children in Wisconsin as his wife had died soon after he enlisted. He had sent his money to them every pay day. He had no bad habits.

As soon as it got dark, they put out pickets in front, two men on a post. Bill Dailey and I were together. Our orders were to crawl out four or five rods, get behind a log or stump, and if we saw the Rebs were getting ready to make an advance, to shoot and get

[4] Frederick B. Mattice, Adams, Jackson County, enlisted October 22, 1861; died April 8, 1865. Edgar P. Houghton said of him, O. P. Graham, and G. W. Reeder: "Company I had three men who ranked high in the regiment as sharpshooters, skirmishers, and foragers. . . . These men were always to be depended upon. Although their guns were not the brightest at inspection, their arms and ammunition were always in good condition when needed. They were counted among the best shots in the regiment. . . . On the skirmish line they were found among those farthest in advance and were the last to fall back. In the riflepits, where they could prove their skill, they were selected for the most difficult work on the line. Graham and Reeder were mustered out with the Company at Mobile, but Mattice was killed in our last battle." Houghton, pp. 45-46.

back to the breastworks as soon as possible. We got behind a log that was too small to be called a log. We had only nicely gotten settled when Bill discovered two Rebs not more than two or three rods from us. They were behind a small log the same as we. Bill wanted to shoot, but I said, "No, they are there to watch us and as long as they keep quiet we are to do the same." We lay there all night watching each other. We could hear them whispering to each other, and I presume they could hear us. But we couldn't hear what they said. As soon as it began to get light in the east, the two Rebs began to crawl toward their works, and we did the same. When I got behind the works, I found I had lost my pocket knife and my bayonet, but I didn't want them bad enough to go after them, although it wasn't over four rods out there.

We were digging trenches day and night and were digging up nearer the fort. We had portholes for the sharpshooters so that when they had their guns in the portholes a bullet couldn't get through. One day I was working digging. There were two to one shovel. We had to keep down on our knees and then keep our heads down, as the Rebs would shoot at the dirt we were throwing out. One rested while the other worked, and while resting would back out into the main trench where a boy that belonged to the Forty-eighth Missouri was sharpshooting. He would stand in front of the porthole and look out of it while loading his gun. I told him he ought to stand to one side as the Rebs were good at shooting and might shoot while he was loading. But he laughed at me, and to show me he wasn't afraid, he jumped up on top of the breastworks and took a shot at the Reb's rifle pits. This was what we called foolhardy, so I saw there was no use talking to him. He was about eighteen years old and a nice-looking young man. That afternoon he was killed by a bullet coming through the porthole.

Fort Blakely was taken, and they marched the prisoners by our camp. We were lined up along the road looking at them when one of the Missouri boys said, "Oh, there comes Jimmy," and he stepped out near the road and said, "Hello, Jimmy." But the Reb never looked up, and when he got near, the Yank plucked at the Reb's elbow. The Reb said, "To hell with you," and wouldn't look at the Yank. The Yank looked as if he had seen a ghost. We all laughed. The Rebs that were near him laughed as well. They were both full-blood Irish, had worked together as deck hands on steamboats, and were neighbors in St. Louis, Missouri. One had no ill feeling, but the other was as mad as a wet hen. He acted as though he was mad at himself and everyone else.

One morning a few days later we found the Rebs in Spanish Fort had given us the slip.[5] They had gotten away in boats during the night and had left the skirmish

[5] According to Grant, Spanish Fort was actually evacuated April 8, 1865, the day before Fort Blakely was captured, and the day before Lee surrendered. *Personal Memoirs*, II, 519.

line as prisoners. There were some small steamboats that ran up the Alabama River as far as Montgomery, Alabama, and they got away on these.

We were soon on the march for Montgomery. On this march we marched through a pitch-pine forest. A big part of the way every tree was boxed. Some trees had three or four boxes. These were chopped in with an axe and would hold a pint of pitch. The pitch was hauled many miles to a distillery camp where it was made into turpentine and tar. The rosin was run out on the ground as waste. There was no underbrush among these pine trees, and they were so scattered there was room to drive a wagon through anywhere. There was no grass. The ground was covered with pine cones. They would burn like pitch, and all we had to do to make a fire was to scratch them together and touch a match to them. But we had to be careful not to let the fire get away, especially if the wind was blowing.

Those in advance would build breastworks. This told us there might be Rebs at any time. But when about halfway to Montgomery we got the news that General Lee had surrendered, and we lay there all day and celebrated.[6] They lined up the artillery of the whole command and fired a gun just about as fast as one could count. An officer sat on a horse at the right of the gun, and he had a small flag called a guidon. Every time he made a motion down, a gun was fired. So the firing was

[6] Houghton (p. 37) says they were camped at the village of Greenville, Alabama, when the news reached them.

as regular as a clock. This sounded nice to us as it was the death knell of secession and meant the cruel war was over.

The next day we resumed the march to Montgomery. We went into camp three miles east of town. We had pickets on the roads to the east of camp, and citizens had to have a pass or be passed by the officer of the guard. They were looking for Jefferson Davis, who was trying to get out of the United States. He was captured not far east of where we were.[7]

[7] At Irwinsville, Georgia, May 11, 1865.

CHAPTER VIII

WAR'S END

The Rebs soon began to pass on their way home, and they were pleased that the war was over. They said they weren't whipped, but were overpowered. And when we got the news that President Lincoln was assassinated, the Rebs appeared to be as sad over it as we were. Minute guns were fired all day the day we got the news, and the flag was at half-mast.

The duty was so light here I used to take long walks out in the country. On one of these walks I came to where some Negroes were harvesting wheat. It was the only wheat I ever saw growing in the Southern states. There were four big buck Negroes cutting with the old turkey-wing cradles. I had never seen this kind of cradle, but had heard of them. The wheat was very thin on the ground, and they caught the wheat off the fingers of the cradle with their left hands at each clip. They often took two clips to get a handful. Then they dropped it on the ground in small piles, two dropping on the same pile. A horde of wenches and children gathered it up into bundles as I had heard my father tell they used to fifty years before. I showed them how we bound in Wisconsin, and they thought it wonderful. But I couldn't show them how to use those cradles. I had never used the cradle at that time.

I saw a house nearly a mile away. They told me it was haunted and that no one had lived in it for a number of years. So I went over to it. It was a large frame house. The windows were gone and the doors open. It was about noon so I lay down on the floor and had a good nap. But the haunts didn't disturb me. I had read of haunted houses in stories, but this was the only one I ever saw. Money wouldn't have hired one of those darkies or the white people there to have lain down and slept there. But now I wasn't afraid of being taken prisoner.

There was no foraging and no need to forage as we got plenty of hardtack and sow belly. The citizens could get a safety guard by taking the oath of allegiance and boarding the guard, and lots of them had a guard. Often these wouldn't let a soldier come in sight before they would halt them. But when the citizens found out we had good money to buy what they had to sell, and that we wanted such things as milk, eggs, butter, and chickens, they brought them to camp to sell. There weren't many men at home, only the very old or cripples. But those who had used their slaves well found that the slaves stayed by them and raised corn, cotton, sweet potatoes, and such without an overseer. The old darkies would consult the missus, and whatever she said was law. Of course, there were lazy, shiftless Negroes, but the older ones would take the lead and they would hunt out the shirkers. The Negroes brought chickens into camp to sell, and the boys asked them to bring milk and eggs, and soon we had a regular delivery.

The whites found out that our greenbacks were the only money that was good in town, so they too began to fetch in truck to sell. One day an elderly man came into camp. He had a two-wheeled dump cart with one horse. He had six or eight bushels of Irish potatoes loose in the cart. They were red and round, about the size of hen's eggs, and he wanted ten cents apiece. Some of the boys were buying them. They were the only Irish potatoes we had ever seen that were raised in the South, so were a rarity. But the boys tried to tell him that was an outrageous price, and finally told him if he couldn't sell them more reasonably, he had better get out of camp. He was defiant, said he would sell his potatoes to suit himself and would get out when he got ready.

He was nearly in front of my tent. There was a big crowd around and he was sitting with his back toward the horse. There was a plug in front to keep the cart box from dumping. Someone pulled out the plug and they hit the horse, and when under good headway, those at the hind end pulled out the end-gate and dumped it at the same time. The man hollered, "Whoa," and began to scramble for the lines. But they were out of reach, and as they dumped the cart he went out with the potatoes, clawing at the sides of the cart. There were enough to see that he came out though, and they piled all over him so that I couldn't see what had become of him. They were rolling him over and over, and when they helped him get up, brushed the dirt off, found his hat, and pretended they had rescued him from the mob, his pockets were wrong side out, and he looked dazed as if he had passed through a cyclone. And there wasn't a potato in sight.

I didn't mix in the mob. I didn't care for the potatoes. I'd rather have sweet potatoes. So I was merely a spectator. But it was a show worth seeing. I felt sorry for the old man, but it really was good enough for him. They ought not to have taken his money. He didn't have anything to say, didn't even thank those that helped him up, or the ones that held his horse, but got in the cart and drove off the most disgusted man I ever saw, and we never saw him again.

The boys got a lot of game roosters. Some fought for money, but the most just for fun. Nearly every tent had a rooster tied to a stake. The men would form a ring so the chickens couldn't get away, and when one rooster was whipped they would fetch another. We had a sergeant, John Rhodus. He was an old batch, forty years old or better, from Kentucky,[1] where they were great sports before the war. John knew a game rooster when he saw one, and he said most of the roosters were common dung-hill fowls. He got a full-blooded game rooster and tied it to his tent stake with quite a long string. One day he was on guard and Adam and Bill

[1] He enlisted from Neillsville, Clark County, Wisconsin, November 7, 1861. Houghton, p. 41.

bought a rooster. It was colored like a Plymouth Rock, but was smaller than the Plymouth Rocks of today. They let him whip John's rooster that was tied up. Then when John got off duty the next day, they told him they had bought a game rooster from a darkey who said it was a good fighter. When John saw it, he laughed at them, and said that darkey had sold them a good one, that that rooster wouldn't fight a little bit. They told him they wouldn't bet, but would fight for fun if he would. He said his rooster would whip that one so quick there wouldn't be any fun to it. So they said, "Fetch on your rooster and we will show you that we are good judges of roosters." So they formed a ring and let the roosters loose, and John's rooster wouldn't fight. John caught his rooster and cut his head off and had chicken for dinner. He never knew the trick they had played on him, but John didn't pose as a judge of game roosters any more, and the boys killed their rooster, as that was all they wanted of it.

Company D got a slim Negro boy ten or twelve years old. He was an expert bucker. He would buck the biggest Negro that walked, and they had lots of fun seeing him buck those big darkies. Some didn't want to buck. Then they would catch and hold the big Negro and let the little darkey hit him once. It was wonderful the way that Negro would hit them. He would stand off some three rods and run and jump just before getting to them, and go head first through the air just like a billy goat. Once was enough for any that came along.

So there was some amusement nearly every day. I saw a little old wench who must have been seventy years old, and wouldn't weigh over one hundred pounds, dance juba after tuckering out about twenty young bucks. She kept on as long as we cared to look on, and said she could dance all day. I believe she could.

I was detailed one day to take charge of a burial squad. It was one of the drafted men. He had died in the hospital about a mile and a half from camp, and his friends wanted to be the escort. I had never performed this, and these men were green at drill. I took them out in the woods and showed them how to go through the performance. These men were all Germans. We had to go to the hospital. We had an ambulance to haul the corpse, and a fifer and drums to furnish the music, and I want to say that is the most solemn music I ever heard. The hospital was a large two-story brick building which was a courthouse, standing all alone a mile from town. It had a basement where they had five dead laid out beside each other. The clerk asked me if I could identify the corpse. I said I thought I could, but I had his neighbors as escort and I would have them identify him. But I had to receipt for it, and this clerk was a brother to my uncle. His name was John Adams and a direct descendant of the Presidents John Adams and John Quincy Adams. He was a few years older than I. We got through the burial ceremony fairly well for a lot of greenhorns.

About this time I got a history of a Spanish explorer

that landed on the coast of Florida with a large command for those days. He had two cannon. I have forgotten most of it, but he was looking for gold, as the Indians had ornaments of gold. They all pointed to the northwest, and as he understood them, there were mountains of it. He passed through where Montgomery is and abandoned one of his cannon there. The history said the cannon was set on the corner of the two principal streets. I had been by that place at least a dozen times and hadn't seen it, so I walked three miles to see that cannon. And there it was, set muzzle down in the ground for a hitching post. It was a brass gun.

He went through Alabama and wintered in Mississippi, where he built a stockade. He was cruel to the Indians who had given him corn until they wouldn't fetch any more corn. Then he captured some of their chiefs and made them fetch corn to ransom the chiefs. He crossed the Mississippi River and struck west when his men began to die with a fever, supposed to be yellow fever. The Indians were getting so thick, and he was finally stricken with the fever, so he turned back to the Mississippi River. There they dug canoes out of big logs to go down the river, but he died before they got the canoes done. They buried him in the river, and the rest went down the river to the Gulf, where he had ordered his ships to be on the lookout for him. They were finally found nearly starved.[2]

[2] This was evidently Hernando de Soto, who landed in Florida in 1539 with a colony of six hundred persons, and was buried in the Mississippi in May, 1542.

It was near the Fourth of July, and all were planning to have something extra for dinner on the Fourth. As our mess looked to me as chief cook, I thought I would get a surprise for them. I had seen some sheep sorrel in an old field and knew it would make sauce similar to pieplant, and had found a mulberry tree that was loaded with berries. They are very much like blackberries, but haven't any seeds. When I went to pick some of them, I found where someone had skinned a hog. It had just been done, and they had cut the legs off near the body, so I took them, scalded and dressed them and made pickled pigs' feet of them. Then I made what my mother called an Indian pudding. This was made of corn meal and a little wheat flour, and I put in mulberries instead of raisins, then put it in a bag and boiled it in a kettle. It had to be hung in the kettle so it wouldn't touch the sides or bottom of the kettle so it wouldn't burn. I had some trouble with this as I got the bag too full and it swelled way beyond my calculations. I had to dig out the middle to keep it from bursting the bag, and it did burst the sack in places all over before it was done clear through, but not enough to spoil the pudding. This was like steamed brown bread. I made a sour gravy to put on it. There were six of us, but that pudding took the eye of all who came along, and all had to have a taste. All called it good, and all said we had the best dinner in camp. None could guess what the sheep sorrel sauce was made of, and the same with the mulberries in the pudding. They made it look nice as well as taste nice.

Our camp was in a large grove of tall trees. One still moonlight night I awoke, and for a little while I couldn't make out just what was going on. There were two owls, one at each end of the grove, and they were making all sorts of noises, scolding back and forth like two old maids. One would gobble away, then the other would break in in a louder key as if mad. Then the other would wait until that one had had the floor long enough. When Nate Clapp,[3] who was sergeant-major, hollered out as though just awake and in a scared tone of voice, "I'll surrender, I'll surrender," everyone was laughing all over camp. All knew Nate's voice, and it broke up the concert of the owls.

We moved down town about this time and camped at the west edge of town. This was the capital of the Confederate States at one time. It was here that Jeff Davis was inaugurated president, but soon moved to Richmond. Soon after we'd moved here, I was detailed to go out on the government plantation, which was fifteen miles east of Montgomery. There were about twelve of us. All belonged to a Michigan regiment except me. There was a sergeant. This plantation had been confiscated from some rebel who had violated his oath or some rules of civil war. There were sixteen hundred acres in the place, but only eight hundred acres cultivated, which was planted to corn. There was a pretty good frame house, five rooms on one floor, and a kitchen

[3] Nathan M. Clapp, Black River Falls, Jackson County, enlisted January 27, 1862. Houghton, p. 39.

separate, about twenty feet from the dining room, with quarters for the house servants. There were about one thousand Negroes, big and little. They were camped in a piece of woods about a half-mile from the house. They had fixed up all kinds of shelter that could be thought of.

The corn was getting quite hard, and we set the darkies to stripping the leaves off for fodder in the place of hay. The corn was planted one stalk in a hill, and it was as high as one could reach on his tiptoes. They would reach up with both hands and strip the leaves from both sides of the stalk with one downward stroke, so on to the next until both hands were full. Then they were bound with a leaf into a bundle and all stuck on the ninth row by doubling the top of a corn stalk over and sticking the small bundle on top where the sun would cure it. This was called the fodder row. When cured, they drove through with a team and gathered the fodder and stacked it around a pole that was set in the ground solid.

Next we went to building log houses for the Negroes. These were covered with shakes about four feet long. They were split out of cypress logs that had been down for ages until the bark and sap or outside were rotted off and moss two inches thick had formed over them. But they were perfectly sound. The butts of these logs for ten to fourteen feet couldn't be split, as the grains were woven together. But from there up it would split like pine. And it resembles pine, but never will rot.

Where this timber grows, the water comes to the top of the ground or above it. So this ground must have been very wet when these were growing. But it was dry now.

We had a nice time the first weeks we were here. One of the boys was about my age. We had two mules to ride, and we explored that country for miles in all directions. One day we went to a house to buy chickens or anything good to eat. But the woman was cranky and spiteful. She didn't want our Yankee money nor anything to do with us. There were no men in sight, and there was a nice little grove of peach trees at one end of the house. The ground under them was covered with peaches and the trees were loaded. We wanted to buy some to eat, but she wouldn't let us have a taste. So I told the boy if he would go with me we would have some, and that night before they were abed we picked peaches by the light of her candle shining through the window. We got about a bushel of the best peaches I ever ate. Probably the way we got them made them taste so good.

Another day we came to a big watermelon patch, twelve acres of them. There was white sand all over the patch that had washed out of the Alabama River near by in high water. The watermelons lay nearly as thick as they could, and were about two feet long. There wasn't a person in sight so we picked the smallest one we saw and took it out in the woods to sample it. We found it O. K., so took a road up through the cornfield that led us to a lot of Negro quarters. The

Negroes seemed to be in full possession, as there weren't any whites around. Along this road were several small patches that appeared to be a later crop. We asked if we could buy some melons, but they said they weren't ripe. I asked them if that was all they had, and they said just a few patches in the corn field. So I said we might as well go back to camp.

One darkey said he had a gun down town to get fixed and he would go with us. He got on an old mule, and I surmised this was an excuse to escort us off the place and see that we didn't find the big patch. So we ran away from the old mule and our dusky friend. There was a big gate to get out to the main road, so we left the gate open and took to one side in the woods to let Mr. Negro pass on to town after his gun. But he shut the gate and went back, thinking they were rid of us. When we were sure he had gone back home, we went and got four melons apiece. That was all we could get in our gunnysacks, and it took both of us to put a sack on a mule.

On the way home we crossed a small pole bridge or culvert. My mule's front feet went through between the poles, and I and the sack of melons went over the mule's head. I landed square on my back and that mule planted a foot on each side of my face and jumped clear over me and the melons. The other fellow caught him, and we loaded up again. It didn't hurt the melons or me.

A few days later we took a mule team and wagon and took some pickled pork and coffee. There were six of us. I rode a mule so as to show them the way. We planned to get there near sundown. Three were to go to the big patch which was off to one side of the road that went to the houses, and if we couldn't trade for melons, we were going to have some anyway. When we asked if they had melons to sell, they said no, they weren't ripe. So I rode up the street until I saw some melons under the bed, and I asked the wench if she would trade them for pork or coffee. She said yes. So when they saw us trading with her, they all had melons and we soon got rid of our pork and coffee.

It was dark by this time, and they took us to the big patch by another road that struck the patch near the north end while our three boys were at the south end carrying them out to the road. While we were loading up what we had bought, the darkies thought they heard someone at the other side. They had a torch to see to pick the melons without tramping the vines. There was a road around the melon patch to the south end and so on out to the main road, and when we had loaded all that we had bought, the team started out that way while I stayed to entertain the darkies.

I kept talking, trying to take their attention from what was going on at the other end of the patch. But they were suspicious, and when they heard the wagon stop, they wanted to know what that wagon stopped for. I said, "Oh, that old harness is more bother than a little. They have to fix it every little way." But I could hear the melons go kerplunk, kerplunk, and the darkies

were bound to go and see "what's de matter." So I put
spurs to my mule and got there first. They had the last
melon in and away we went. We didn't stop to shut
the gate as we went into the road, but I lagged behind
for a mile or two to see if they were following. So we
had melons until we were tired of them.

One day we went to see the Negroes catch fish with
a seine they had made out of grape vines. It was about
fifty feet long and five feet deep. The pond was a low
place where the river overflowed in high water, and the
water was about five feet deep in the middle. It was
about one hundred feet across and nearly round. They
were getting a lot of gar fish. They were some two feet
long, and looked like fish until you got to the head
which looked like an alligator head. They said they
were good to eat, but we took their word for that. But
they had a spoonbill catfish that would weigh about ten
pounds dressed. We gave them a dollar for it. We knew
that was good as the old Negro mammy we had to cook
for us fried that fish to a nice brown. She was a good
cook if she was rather dark complected, and she always
had our meals on time right to the dot, and everything
was neat and clean.

There was a grove of large timber about half a mile
from the house. It was surrounded with the corn field,
and we heard turkeys gobble there nearly every morning. The boy of my age and I cut some lead up into
slugs and loaded our guns and went out to the grove
before daylight thinking we would have turkey for

dinner. But although we were as still as we could be, we never saw or heard a turk, and we went out several mornings. We thought they had roosted somewhere else those nights, but if we didn't go we would hear them gobble out there. So from what I read of them years after, I am sure they heard and perhaps saw us coming and would slip out when we went out there. And in the nearly four years I was in the South, I never saw a wild turkey either dead or alive, although they were all over the South at that time.

We had a fine time until a captain from a Missouri regiment came out and took command. He was nice to us for a time but soon began to show the brute that he was. First he was going to educate the young Negroes, and he had a class come up every day to learn the alphabet. One boy about fifteen years old soon learned the letters, so he thought he knew the whole thing and he didn't think there was any use of his coming any more. This riled the captain, so he had the boy fetched up and stretched out on his back on the lawn. Had his hands tied to stakes, also his feet tied to stakes, and the sun beating down on his face, and the captain sat on the porch in the shade and tantalized him and gloated over his way of punishment.

Then he got a young mockingbird and had it in a canary bird cage, hung on the porch. He had a mulatto girl about fifteen years old to take care of the bird and his room. She had to hunt cutworms for the bird. But the bird died and he said the girl didn't half feed it, and when she came to sweep his room he kicked her out most brutally. We had ought to have let him know then what we thought of him, but he was our superior officer. But I think he could see we did not like his brutal ways.

An old darkey came along with some young hound pups and the captain took one and put it in the bird cage. The little pup began to cry and whine for its mother. Its tail stuck out of the cage, and the captain cut a piece off its tail. He kept cutting off a piece at a time until its tail was all cut off. He would gloat over it, and say he didn't like a nigger hound, as though he thought it cunning to torment that little puppy.

Finally he got a doctor to come out there with a small drug store, and they needed the whole house for headquarters. They had a log house built for us near the Negro quarters. He had a saddle horse and an orderly to take care of it, and he had his orderly to fetch us his orders. One order was that we should go out with our Negroes to work when the horn blew. The horn was an old conch shell he had gotten somewhere, and the orderly would ride down from headquarters to blow it. This was too much for me. We hadn't gotten our bunks made in the log house, and had slept two nights on the floor, so I said, "I am going to finish my bunk before I go out to work." Several of the boys said they wouldn't go until I did. The orderly stopped to see if we went after he blew the horn and so went and reported as the captain had ordered.

Soon the boys said, "Here comes the captain."

He had his revolver and belts on and he rode up in front of our house. The door was open and he began God-damning us to get out to work.

I went to the door and asked him, "Who are you damning?"

He said, "I want you to go to work when that horn is blown."

I said, "You can't damn me unless you are a better man than I am, so if you will get off that horse and take off that coat, we'll see which is the best man," and I went out to him. He said he didn't come for a row.

But I said, "What did you think, that you could scare us with that gun strapped to your hip? If so, you are barking up the wrong tree."

He said he had just come in from his morning ride, and when the boy told him we hadn't gone to work, he didn't stop to take his belt off.

So I said, "I am not going to work until I get my bunk made, and I want you to know I am an American, and you can't make a nigger nor a slave out of me." So he rode off.

The boys said, "He will have you court-martialed for disrespect to an officer."

I said, "He had no right to damn us, and I don't believe he dare have us arrested."

The old conch shell wasn't blown any more while we were there, but we were relieved in a few days by a detail from his regiment. We told them about the "jaw suit," and they said they wouldn't be made to go and come by his conch shell. So we went to our regiment.

My regiment had gone to Mobile, Alabama, and I went there. The regiment was camped in the western suburbs about a mile from the bay. The duty was very light, just patrolling the city. There was a regiment of Negroes that was camped in the southern edge of the city, and a regiment of regulars came and camped near us. They [the regulars] put a camp guard around their regiment. They soon had two men hung up by the thumbs, and the way they screamed was something awful. This was something new to us, and soon our boys went up near their camp guard line and began hollering to take those men down, and finally said, "If you don't take them down, we will take them down and lick every officer there." There was a number of officers standing around apparently bossing the job, but the men were taken down.

But their colonel outranked ours, and he ordered our colonel to put a camp guard around our regiment. So the guard was put on, and Adam Relyea was corporal of the first relief. On the back side of camp was our colonel's stable outside of the guard line. There was one man, his name was Corbet, was kind of a gawky-looking fellow. At one end of his beat there was a nice shade tree. His orders were to walk his beat and salute all officers, and not let any privates out without a pass, but let all come in. Adam saw him sit down in the shade and take his gun apart and go to cleaning it. Adam stood near, as he knew the colonel was over at his horse barn. Soon the colonel came along. He stopped and looked at Corbet. Corbet never looked up, but was busy cleaning his gun. So the colonel asked him what were his orders.

"My orders are to clean my gun and shoot all officers," said Corbet.

"Well," said the colonel, "I will get out of sight before you get that gun together."

So everybody went to town.

The regulars put up a guardhouse, just single boards, and hung men up in there. We could hear them scream, and our boys told the regulars they would tear down the guard house and lick the officers that came near (this to be done after dark), and if they undertook to fetch the Negroes up, our regiment would stand them off. And after dark they did tear down the guardhouse. But their officers were wise enough to keep at a distance, and the next day they moved to the other side of the city.

We used to go down to the bay a little south of the city where there was the hull of quite a large boat that had been beached and burned to the water's edge some years before. The wind and waves shoved it nearly half onto the beach, and the rudder was near two feet out or above the water at low tide. The boys used to swim out to it and climb out on it to dive off as the water was deep out there. I never went swimming here as I wasn't feeling well, but used to sit and see sometimes

twenty-five of the boys in, and a few years after I saw
in the paper a picture of the old hull and an account of
a man being in swimming when a shark got after him
and he climbed on the rudder of the old hull, but as
he was climbing on it, the shark bit one of his legs off.

About this time they gave us the worst rations of
hardtack and pork. The hardtack was alive with little
black bread bugs. They had bored it full of holes and
one couldn't get them all out. You could tell when you
ground them up as they were bitter. The pork was
rotten, with maggots in it. So I told the boys if they
would throw in and get some flour, I would make bread.
We had to get an order from the captain for his mess,
and the boys went down town to the post commissary.
The commissary wouldn't let them have it, said the
captain was getting too much for his mess. So I said I
would go down and see them. So I went down and said,
"You give me that flour or I will go to headquarters and
see about it." He went to dishing out the flour, but was
shooting off his mouth. I told him, "You are issuing con-
demned rations to us and you know that nobody can
eat them, and somebody is lining his pockets out of it."

So this made me late with my bread, and when I got
it baked it was after midnight and I was tired and warm
and went and lay down without covering up. I caught
cold and never tasted that bread. And for about thirty
days I had the malarial fever. It rained nearly every day.
It would rain just a minute and then the sun would
shine. The doctor wanted me to go to the hospital, but

I didn't want to go. He said if I didn't go I would die, so I said I would go, and the ambulance came and took another man and me up to the hospital. But they would not put me in, so I was sent back, and the old doctor was mad. He came over to my tent and said, "Now you keep a stiff upper lip and I will do everything I can for you." He used to come three or four times a day. I got so weak I couldn't turn over on the bunk without help, and don't think I would have lived if it hadn't been for the care Adam Relyea gave me. But my time hadn't come, and the ninth of October we were discharged at Mobile. I was better. The chills and fever had left, and I gained strength fast, but was a skeleton. The thought of once more going back to God's country was the best medicine I could get.

I told the boys I wanted to bake some bread so we could have something besides hardtack on the way up the river. So they got some flour, and I made bread and about a half-bushel of fried cakes like my mother used to make, by cutting the dough in strips and twisting it together. I sweetened them a little too much. Adam made a mess chest or box to carry our grub in. The fried cakes commenced to spoil before we got them all eaten up. When we would break one in two, it would look as if it had hairs in it. This was the first stage of mold, but we didn't let them get in the second stage. We had been saving them to make them last. They tasted good, though we didn't like the looks of those hairs, and I didn't break what I ate to see if it had hairs as my stomach wasn't as good as when I fried the fish on the Atlanta campaign. These were the only fried cakes I ever made, and I used a beer bottle for a rolling pin.

The next day we boarded the same old side-wheel steamer we had come over to Dauphin Island on in the spring, and went back up Lake Pontchartrain. It was dark when we got on the lake and had all lain down to sleep. The wind blew down the lake so as to make pretty big waves, and that old boat cracked as though it was breaking in two, and I could feel it bending up and down as we were on the upper deck and near the middle. My stomach began to roll with every motion of the boat, so I got up and got hold of the railing back of the pilot house, and the cool wind in my face soon fixed me good.

There were some of the other companies down on the lower deck, and one of those men got up and walked off the boat just in front of the big paddle wheel that propelled the boat. They stopped as soon as possible and lowered a boat and hunted for an hour, but didn't find him. They put a guard there so no more could get off there. But I don't think there was any more sleep on that boat that night.

We got to the landing just at peep of day, and we marched across to New Orleans where we got on board a steamboat. Charley Stahl, whom I have spoken of before who was with the Rebs at Shiloh and had been discharged in June after serving three years in the Union Army, came down to the boat to see us, and he was a big fat Dutchman. We were glad to see him. This was the last I ever heard of him.

We went up to Cairo, where they put us in box and cattle cars that hadn't been very well cleaned out and had no straw or hay for bedding. We were so crowded that all had to lay on the same side, and our legs were mixed with the row on the other side of the car. But there was but little fault found for we were going home. "Why, boy, the thought filled every heart with joy for those happy homes for which we fought that traitors would destroy."

We finally got to Freeport, Illinois, and we found on waking Sunday morning we were on a side track without an engine. There was a passenger coach for the commissioned officers to ride in. The box cars had no springs on them, and that engineer seemed to delight in jerking them back and forth, not letting them stand still a minute. Some of the boys would swear and call him names, but that didn't help. We were an extra and had to wait for all other trains, so we were two days and nights from Cairo to here, but we had gotten here in the middle of the night sometime and had a good sleep until morning.

About nine o'clock a brand new engine came and hitched onto us. It was the first engine we had seen with a small smokestack, and it looked so small it was a curiosity. A lot of the boys went to look at it, and some would ask fool questions. They asked the engineer if it could run. He said it could go some. They told him they had walked all the way from Cairo, and they would like to have a ride. He said, "You will ride from here to Beloit. That is as far as I go." It being Sunday, there were no other trains so we had a clear track, and, say, we did ride! A lot of the boys got on top of the cars and we had the doors open. But those on top soon got inside, and we had to shut the doors to keep the smoke and cinders out, and finally had to sit down, as one couldn't stand up. It seemed as if he went faster all the time. And when we got to Beloit, they went up and thanked him for the ride, and wished he would take us clear home.

When we got to Beloit, the ladies had a swell dinner for us and a nice place to wash. And we sure needed the wash as we hadn't washed since leaving New Orleans. After dinner we were lined up and the colonel proposed three cheers for the ladies of Beloit, and they were given with a will, and the tiger as well.

We were soon on our way to Madison, this time in clean new box cars. In Madison we were put in a large building, but I with others got in hotels or private boardinghouses. I got in with John Shehan, whom I had stayed with when here before on furlough. He was chief of police.

In a few days we were paid off and given our discharge, and each went his way a free American citizen once more. No one who hasn't been a soldier for several years of cruel war can know the joy and freedom we felt to go and come as we pleased, and not be domineered over by an officer. But I will say we had the most lenient officers in the army.

This ends my experience. I haven't told all, but what I have is the truth to the best of my recollections.

STOCKWELL'S LETTERS
TO HIS PARENTS

Reproduced here are six of the letters which Elisha Stockwell, Jr., wrote home during the time he was in the army. Obviously many more were written, but it has been possible at this time to locate only the six which follow.

No attempt has been made to edit these letters in any way, and they are reproduced here as faithfully as possible, with exactly the punctuation, spelling, grammar, and word usage of the originals. While editing might have added to their readability, it was felt that it would tend to destroy their personality.

St. Louis
March the 12th, 1862

Respected parents,

I take my pen in hand to let you know that I am well and where I am. We are on the fair ground. I rote you a letter the 7th of March. if you want to rite to me you can. We got here the day before yesterday all hale and sound. we are about 5 miles from the Mississippi River at Benton baracks. As we was a coming through Illinois by railroad they catched two rebbels atrying to burn a R.R. bridge and they took them prisoners and brot them to St. Louis and put them in prison. there is seventeen Regiments here in the bareks and in camp here on the grounds. It is very warm here and is very dry to boot. there is some mud here yet. we marched through Schoggo [Chicago] the mud was over shoe all of the way through. I guess that I can stand as much as a good many other soldiers. Edgar and Harrison Maxon had the headache two nights and one day after we got here. they are getting pretty strict here. the cornel can't pass the guard without the counter sign or a pass. The cavlery at Benton Barack have 10 brass pieces of field artillary. Well, I must hold on for they are agoing to drilling so goodby for just now. Direct your letters to Com I—14th Reg. Wis Volenteers, St. Louis, Missouri.

March the 30th, 1862

Dear Mother,

I received your letter today and as it rains I thought I would rite a few lines to you. I am well except I have a bad cold but it is getting better. we are at Savannah now. we got here last Friday. we had a long bote ride. We came down the Mississippi and up the Ohio and then Tennessee. the farms along the Ohio River was a good many under watter. some of the houses was half under watter and the folks was in the houses yet it looked kinda queere. some plases the folks had left the plases all except the niggers they had left niggers to take care of the things. there was a nigger come in here yestarday to report their master he has come back after their niggers. I stood picket guard last night. the weather is very warm here and the ground is very dry. there is a good many peach trees here and they are all in bloom. they look nice. I don't like the weather here as well as up there. how does Adelaid get along and what has she named her boy. how does the old mair get along. It is amusing to see the men drive mules. they drive six mules on a bagage wagon. The hind right mule wears the saddle. the driver rides in the saddle and drives the six mules with one line attached to the forward mule. you don't know anything about the nigers in the south. there has one family which have to pack stuf for the soldiers and take such stuff as the soldiers don't want for pay. how does Frank get along? what is Miss Pomroy a doing. I would like to get hold of one of Miss Pomroy's pies. Well, I must stop for my supper, so goodby for this time.

In Camp Near Vicksburg, July 8th, 1863
Respected mother,

I received a letter from you some time ago and have answered it, but I thought I would write a few lines to you to let you know that I got into Vicksburg at last alive and well. we came in on the day of the 4th of July. We had a happy fourth you may bet. we came in with Logan's division. the stars and stripes were hoisted on the court house and we marched down on main street in front of the court house and gave three cheers for the flag of our union. we stayed in town until night and then went back to our old camping ground. we lay a little east of north from the town up the river from the town about a mile from town. we have considerable guard duty to do now, but I don't think that it will be so heavy when we get rid of these prisoners they are paroling them as fast as they can. there is lots of them that wont take a parole. they want to get out of it the most of the Tennessee troops will take the oath of alegiance and a good many of the Mo. troops will take the oath too. I wrote to George Heaydon the 3rd of July. I told him that there was a flag of truce then, but we did not know what it was for and that if I found out before I sent it away, it was to know what conditions Pemberton would surrender on. Well, I am glad that it is over with. what was going on up there the fourth. I hope that you enjoyed yourself as well as I did. it was the happiest fourth that I ever spent, and it was so unexpected that it made a great difference. they say that they had rather Pemberton would surrender on any other day than the fourth. they could not stood it two days longer anyhow for they had issued the last rations that they had in there.

Does Will go to school this summer and Dell? I would like to step in and see them some day. I don't think that they would know me now.   as soon as I get a chance I am going to get my picture taken and send it home.   Well I must stop for this time so good by. give my best respects to all.

Elisha Stockwell, Jr.

In Camp Eastport Miss. Jan. 16th 1865

Dear Mother

It is with pleasure that I sit down to answer your kind letter of Dec. 18th as it is the first letter I have received since I got Father's letter.   well Mother I am a little under the weather at present.   I have got a bad cold and the diarea but nothing very serious.   I will tell you how we have been used and then you will not wonder that I have a cold.   after we left Nashville Tenn. we marched all the time on graveled pike and my shoes was nearly wore out when we started and we have not had a chance to draw clothing until about a week ago.   well the consequences was that I had to march about 125 miles barefooted and in the time we had 4 snow storms of 3 or 4 inches at a time.   I marched one day that I left blood in my tracks every step but I made them carry my traps.   So you can judge for your self the kind of times that we have had after Old Hood.   we drawed clothing about a week ago and started on a march the next morning.   we marched from this place to Corrinth Miss. and turned and came back 12 miles in two days.   it is about 35 miles from here to Corrinth.   the most of us had new shoes and if ever there was a lot of stiff chickens it was us. Corrinth is all burned down. we went out on a scout there was one brigade of rebs there at Corrinth the night before we got there but they thought the whole army was coming through that way so they thought they would get in our rear and pick up stragelers in sted of that they run into our advance when we was comming back we took quite a number of prisoners. the country as far as we went is completly destroyed it dont look like the same place that it did 2 years ago. O Mother you had ought to see us bying stuff at our sutlers. I will give you some of his prices Butter 80 cts pound cheese 60 dried apples 40 molasses $1.00 quart onions 25 cts a pound. Cranberry sauce 1 doll a can the cans will almost a pint. boots 15 dollars a pair and everything in proportion. you wanted to know if I got that tobacco that Ad. sent me. I did and darned glad I was to get it at the time. for we was where we could not get any and I was entirely out. wanted to know what tobacco was a pound. I have not bought any lately because I have quit using it. but the price of chewing comon plug tobacco is $2.00 a pound smoking 1 doll for 12 ounces. you wanted to know if you could send anything in safety to me I think you could by sending it in Capt. Michal Crawleys name. there is no express agent here now but I think there will be one here before long. we are expecting to stay here the rest of the winter. I would thank Uncle Sam very much if he would come down and see us with a few green Backs but I suppose that he will take his own time for it so there is no use of grumbling about it.

Well Mother what are you going to have for supper if you are agoing have a better supper than I am I will eat mine then. all under the heavens and earth we have got the last two days is a pint of sheld corn to each man and we do not know when we will get any thing else. So you may judge for yourself whether we are fatting or not. I have not received any letters from Adelaid in nearly a month. I am agoing to write agin in a day or tow. I got a letter from aunt Adelaid the other day. she was well but said that they had a good deal of custom and it kept her pretty busy. no more at present give my love to the children and tell Willie to take care of that Jackknife I gave him. this from your son

Elisha Stockwell

> direct to Wards Brig.
> Gen. Kilby Smiths Division
> Detatchment Army. Tenn.

I will send you a piece of our old regamental flag that has been in all the Battles with the 14th I tried to get a biger peice but could not.

[With the above letter was also enclosed the following poem, which apparently had been cut out of some paper or magazine.]

> *When the glorious orb of day,*
> *Shines to light and cheer the way,*

Private Elisha Stockwell, Jr., Sees the Civil War

> *Or the twinkling stars of night,*
> *Shall reflect their feeble light—*
> *'Though in a far distant land*
> *Think upon an absent friend.*
> *Sure, I shall remember thee,*
> *Though far distant we may be!*
> *Memory oft shall bring thee near,*
> *Calling forth a silent tear;*
> *Oft that welcome guest shall say,*
> *"Think of one that's far away!"*

New Orleans La March 8th 1865

Dear Mother.

I reseived your kind letter of Feb 12th which arived last night. I was verry glad to hear from you once more and to hear that you was well and having such good times. I am well and pretty tough again. our division is here yet but the other two divisions of our Corps has gone down the river somewhere we dont know where nor we don't know but we will go next. I hope we will for I have layed here in the mud long enough it makes a business of raining here and we are laying on a flat where the wind has got a fair chance at us for about 5 or 6 miles. there came up a storm night before last and I thought for a few minutes it would blow us clear into the air. but we made out to stick to the arth. last night I hunted an old cotten mouth Snake out of my tent he was about 5 feet long. them and the lizards make nice bed felows the other morning I woke up and got up and found that I had layed on a lizard untill I had killed him.

We havnot got payed off yet. I have made up my mind to go without pay untill the war is ended. well it was a wise thing for me that I quit using tobacco when I got out for I would had to give it up after a while any how. you wanted to know if there was any more in the regt. that was barefooted when I was there was plenty of them that was nearly as bad as I was and some worse but that is over and I am glad for one that it is. I'll bet you would laugh if you was here this morning and see me making pooding out of hardtack but I made a pretty good one it went first rate if I had had some raisins to put into it it would have improved it I think.

I got a letter from Adelaid the other day she was well when she wrote she said she had to do the housework all alone. I think she is darned foolish to do it but evry one to their notion as the old woman said when she kissed the cow. Nick had sold his saloon and was going to buy another one If he could raise the money. I supose that you have got the bundle that I sent from Cairo before this time there was 1 wool Blanket a pair of pants and a shirt and I supose that Frank is almost a foot taller if Jim Baty has got up into that country yet.

I started a bundle the 27th of Febuary from here there was two Blankets 4 overcoats one shirt and two pair Drawers. I would sent more but I did not know how much it would cost to express them if I had had the money to payed down for the things and paid the expressage I would have sent more. I havnot been down town yet. if I got my pay here I was calculating to go down town and get one meal of oysters but I would not give a snap to go just to see the place. I was in the monument that they have comenced to build in memory of the Battle that old Jackson fought. I should think it was about 70 foot high you go in side to go to the top of it there is 87 steps in the stairs and they wind 4 times around the senter it is built of Brick but it looks on the out side as if it was built of stone. give a Brothers love to the children and a Sons and soldiers love to Father and mother.

Elisha Stockwell

direct to Co. I. 14th Wisconsin Vet. Vol. 1st Brigade & division 16th Ar. C. Via Cairo Ill.

In camp in the Field. March 31,st 1865

Dear Mother,

It is with pleasure that I take my pen to answer your letter of the 2nd March. I do not get much time to write. I wrote you last from New Orleans, La. since then we marched to Lake Ponchartrain took the steamer and went to Dauphin Island where we lay about two weaks. the Iland looks at a distance as iff it was a snow Bank it is white sand. we had a first rate time while we was there we used to go out and hunt oyesters we could go out about half a mile from shore and pick up all the oysters we want to. I did wish that I could hand some into mother but I know that I could not so I ate about two quarts for you that was the best I could do. them was the first raw oyesters that I ever ate. But they went down as though they were greased. what a Soldier cant eat no one else nead to try to. I saw them eating mussels raw and raw frogs and catching these fresh watter crabs and eating the pinchers. you may think I am joking but I am not. wait untill I eat my diner and I will finish. well I have eat my dinner which consisted of a cup of coffee one hard tack and a slice of Bakon or what the Soldier calls Sow Belly. I guess that if I Stay in the army much longer I will haf to get a new set of teeth my teeth have roted for the last two months awful fast but they dont ake a lote but it bothers me to eat hardtack considerable. but I can make out to eat all I draw. I got a letter from Adelaid Jarvis the other day. She was well. I guess that there is a good show for us to pass another Summer without pay for my part I dont like it a tall I think that they might just as well payed us off at New Orleans as not to. but we will have the more when it comes I have just 12 months pay comming to me today Besides 3 installments of Bounty, well since we left the Iland we have been on the move we came up Fish river to fresh landing and marched across to Fort Spanish which we are seiging now it is right acrost the Bay from Mobeil we can see Mobeil plain from our Fort on the right or left. Our Gun Boats are fishing torpeadoes and making their best way up the Bay it is reported that Thomas is comming up in the rear of Mobeil with 30 thousand men. I know that our train went with provision to the Gen Steele he is about 30 miles from here and out of rations but I dont know where he is.   tell Frank that I will answer his letter as soon as I get a chance but they keep us to work nearly all of the time.   and the Johnneys drive us into our holes Just when they take a notion to. You said that frank talked of Enlisting if he knows when he is well off he had better stay to home he will find diferent funn than he is looking for if he was a few years older I would encourage him in enlistin But I think he will do more good to home raising murphys and sowbelly.   I just got a letter from Philotus Hayden he was well.   maby you will wonder that I havenot wrote Before But we could not send mail away so I didnot write.

excuse all bad wrighting and spelling.

Elisha Stockwell
Company I 14th Reg.

INDEX

Index